SURVIVING OPPRESSION

GOOD PEOPLE
BAND TOGETHER

BY BILL SCHULTZ

TABLE OF CONTENTS

Large numbers of strangers can cooperate
successfully by believing in common myths.

== Yuval Noah Harari

PREFACE

This book was inspired by the writings of the German historian, philosopher, and polymath Oswald Spengler.[1] Over a century ago Spengler wrote a two-volume book in German.[2] The English title was *The Decline of the West*.[3] Spengler's prose is difficult to read, partly because most readers don't have the background knowledge of many of the disciplines he writes about. Spengler obtained his Doctor of Philosophy degree from a German university that was very "old school" because it required a breadth of knowledge in numerous areas before such a degree was granted.[4] Spengler's book illustrates his ideas by citing numerous examples from diverse fields such as art, music, history, philosophy, mathematics, politics, and religion. Few people have the diversity of knowledge necessary to understand all those fields.

Spengler began writing in 1911, completing Volume I in 1914, but he did not publish it until just before the end of World War I in 1918. This timing contributed to the massive success of the first volume as it seemed to describe precisely what led to the national humiliation of Germany during the negotiations for the 1919 Treaty of Versailles.

Another part of what makes Spengler difficult to read is his redefinition of certain words which have different meanings in ordinary usage. An ordinary person understands the word "civilization" to mean the entire sweep of history for a particular people, while Spengler restricts that word to refer to only the latter part of that history, after a particular turning point. For Western history, that turning point was around 1800

---

[1] Oswald Spengler, born May 29, 1880, died May 8, 1936. After his writings were greatly mis-used by the Nazis, he was largely written out of Western history and scholarship. My mother, born in 1918, learned some of his ideas in her high school in Los Angeles in the early 1930s. But by the time I went to high school in the early 1960s, there were no mentions of Spengler or his ideas.

See https://en.wikipedia.org/wiki/Oswald_Spengler for his biography.

[2] The German title was *Der Untergang des Abendlandes*. Volume I was published in 1918, and Volume II was published in 1922.

[3] The English publication for Volume I was on April 23, 1926, and for Volume II it was on November 9, 1928. The English translation was by Charles Francis Atkinson (1880-1960).

[4] In a way, the failure of modern PhD programs of scholarship to enforce a true requirement of breadth of knowledge is part of the overall decline of western education, which runs along with the decline of the overall civilization.

with the rise of Napoleon. Spengler called the period before Napoleon "Culture" and the period beginning with Napoleon "Civilization." The Culture period so overlaps the history of the Holy Roman Empire (800-1806) that we might easily choose to assign the beginning and end dates of that empire to the beginning and end of the Culture period in the West. It began on December 25, 800 CE.[5] And it ended August 6, 1806 CE.[6] I will use the word "society" to refer to the entire sweep of "the West" in human history, both "Culture" and "Civilization."

The descriptive label of "the West" derives from the Western Roman Empire, seated in Rome, Italy. That empire came to an end in the fifth century, sometimes stated as 476 CE.[7] Italy had no effective monarchy until Charlemagne was crowned in 800 CE. Meanwhile, the Eastern Roman Empire evolved into the Byzantine Empire (330-1453) seated in Constantinople (modern-day Istanbul).[8] The Islamic Ottoman Empire took the city and all of Byzantium in 1453.

Spengler's primary metaphor is that the West rises and grows during the Culture period and declines and falls during the Civilization period, which is a pattern he claims for all the great societies that he studied.[9] Thus, the decline of the West begins with Napoleon.[10] It continues as far into the future as "the West" might continue to exist. The only way that "the West" ends is if it is in some way destroyed or replaced.

The declining Western Civilization is bad for most people. While a few wealthy people can achieve happiness in this environment, most of the population struggles to live a decent life. A 2004 article on

---

[5] This is the date that the Emperor Charlemagne was crowned "Emperor of the Romans" by Pope Leo III.

[6] This is the date that the Emperor Francis II abdicated and dissolved the Holy Roman Empire as ordered by Napoleon. He did this to avoid a wider war. Francis retained his other titles as King and Emperor of other nations, in particular he remained the Emperor of Austria and of the Austro-Hungarian Empire.

[7] This date is disputed. Others date the fall of the Western Roman Empire to the 455 sacking of Rome by a Vandal army.

[8] The city of Constantinople was founded by the first Emperor of the East, Constantine I, who renamed the earlier city of Byzantium after himself. See https://en.wikipedia.org/wiki/Constantinople for more.

[9] Again, I am using the word "society" where most people would use the word "civilization" because Spengler uses the word "civilization" in a special sense to refer only to the later part of the history of a given society.

[10] The "cultural contemporary" (a Spenglerism) of Napoleon is Alexander the Great, not any of the Caesars.

population trends summarizes Spengler's opinion of our current state where the more advanced nations are losing population.[11] The 2004 article says this about Spengler:[12]

> *[Spengler describes] the morphology of urban forms and of the rise of the world city.[13] As longer-term consequences (... "between 2000 and 2200") Spengler foresaw the "formation of Caesarism"; "victory of force-politics over money"; "increasing primitiveness of political forms"; and "inward decline of the nations into a formless population, and constitution thereof as an Imperium of gradually increasing crudity and despotism."[14]*

Spengler would view leaders like Donald Trump not as an aberration, but as the predicted consequence of the aforementioned historical trend which has been building since the very foundation of Western society in 800 CE. In my view, Trump can be compared to Nero.[15] He was a Roman Emperor who was viewed as a bumbling fool in certain ways. Even so, Nero was very consequential in the history of Rome, as Trump will be in the history of the United States.

---

[11] In general, more primitive nations increase population, more advanced nations less so, with the most advanced nations exhibiting declining population. Two decades later those trends are even more obvious than they were in 2004.

[12] The recent writing cites to *Decline of the West*, Volume II, Perspective of World History, Chapter IV, The Soul of the City, Section V, where Spengler discusses the unacknowledged pressure to reduce population.

[13] Spengler uses words like "form" and "formless" in a particular sense. A population is "in form" if it is fit for the particular purpose which Spengler assigns to that time in the history of the society. A good leader leads his people to be "in form" and to fulfill the destiny of the society at that time and place. Thus, a "formless population" is a disorganized mass of people who cannot be so led. That includes one like our current situation in the United States where the people are divided into two halves who are bitter enemies in nearly every respect.

[14] The quote comes from the online Abstract of the article in Population and Development Review with the title "Oswald Spengler on Cosmopolis and Depopulation," first published 27 January 2004. See https://onlinelibrary.wiley.com/doi/10.1111/j.1728-4457.2002.00787.x for the source of this quote.

[15] Nero Claudius Caesar Augustus Germanicus (born Lucius Domitius Ahenobarbus, 15 December, 37 CE, died 9 June 68 CE). The comparison doesn't really hold because the West probably hasn't had a Julius Caesar, a great unifying leader who begins an era of absolute dictatorship. The only real candidate in 2025 would be Putin of Russia.

It seems the West is experiencing "increasing crudity and despotism." It isn't just Trump. It's Modi in India, Orbán in Hungary, Lukashenko in Belarus, Putin in Russia, and Xi in China.[16]

They are all moving their western-type societies towards "increasing crudity and despotism." And major nations within the West are experiencing declines of their non-immigrant populations, which are in some nations offset by immigration from "3rd world" nations.

In some sense we might say that the West is rapidly going to Hell in a handbasket.[17] The argument over using that phrase would be the word "rapidly." In terms of an individual human being, it may not seem to be happening rapidly. But in terms of multi-millennia historical trends, it is happening rapidly. And the driving force for the decline of the West cannot be reversed. The West can only be replaced or not replaced. That is our choice. We can either continue to experience the decline of the West or we can choose to replace it and build something new.

When I was far enough along with writing this book that I began to think about publishing it I began to look at companies who offered solutions to my needs. One prospective publisher offered a guide for authors that asked me to think about "Why" I am writing a book in the first place, and that my "Why" would inform many aspects of the writing. I was asked to dig deep into why I was writing this book. In my case, I have a big, bold, even outlandish "Why." I want the people of the world to take a giant left turn away from the West.[18] It is declining into "an Imperium of gradually increasing crudity and despotism." Instead we should begin a transition to a completely new society (Culture followed by Civilization, in Spengler's terms), which will be the very

---

[16] China is "Western" because it's philosophical foundation is the German writings of Marx and Engels. Similarly, India was westernized during several centuries of English occupation and control. To train civil servants, England established a wide network of English schools, which then trained the Indian scholars in the basics of western Culture.

[17] "… an idiom that means a situation is rapidly deteriorating or heading towards complete disaster, essentially implying something is quickly going downhill and cannot be salvaged; it's often used to describe a situation that seems inescapable and headed for ruin." (Google AI definition.)

[18] If the movement towards authoritarianism, or even fascism, can be seen as a "right turn" for society, then I want to turn away from that. Thus, the "left turn" is towards a more socialistic society where people care more for each other, with particular emphasis on family, friends, neighbors, and the larger circles of our individual societies.

first intentionally designed society of humans. This has never been done before, not even within the Eastern Roman Empire.[19] Past societies (Cultures, Civilizations, etc.) have ended after military conquests by outside societies or dissolved through their internal processes (like some Mesoamerican societies). But none has ever been deliberately replaced by a better idea. Essentially, I'm telling the 8 billion people of Earth to march this way, not that way. That's an audacious "Why," isn't it?

If you feel like you're stuck in that handbasket headed to Hell, as I feel myself, then you should ask "what can I do?" With 7,999,999,999 people headed in the wrong direction, how much can one person do to point them all in the opposite direction? My answer is to write this book and see how many of those 8 billion feel the way I do: **We must go a different way.**

And the next step is to gather those who are willing to change direction into a movement designed to build up the society which we design for ourselves. I would never claim to have all the answers. There must be thousands of people out there who have better ideas than I have about one thing or another. Modern technology gives us the Internet.[20] That allows us to collaborate almost without regard to our location.[21] I have some experience as a web server administrator, and I will establish some basic websites to begin a conversation. But if you have a better idea, don't hesitate to set up your own web presence, or to at least join mine. We can use all the help we can get.

Every society (culture, civilization) begins with a religion. It can change religion later, or it can become more diverse and accept multiple religions. But the key to binding together a society at the beginning is to have a single common religion. The West began, somewhat

---

[19] There was an unplanned flow into a new Empire which was only called Byzantine by later historians.

[20] On occasion I tell a joke that I helped Al Gore invent the Internet. (From an out-of-control claim Gore made during his 2000 campaign for President. Gore wrote a bill telling DARPA to pursue the goal and provided funding.) I was involved much later. In the mid-1970s, two decades before the Internet was released to the public, I had an account on Arpa Net, the predecessor to the public Internet.

[21] The Great Firewall of China, and similar restrictions by other authoritarian nations, restricts participation by people located within those oppressive nations. If some communication in and out is allowed, we can hope that some kinds of VPN technologies will keep us all in touch.

accidentally, with Christianity. Christianity had been established in the late Roman Empire by the Emperor Constantine. When the Western Roman Empire fell in the 5th century, it left the Roman Catholic Church operating in Rome and making conversions among the uncivilized tribes throughout Western Europe. The Franks converted to Christianity around the beginning of the 6th century, so when Charles Martel defeated the Islamic invaders in 732, it was a Christian army against an Islamic army.[22] If the Islamic army of the Umayyad Caliphate had prevailed, Western Civilization would not exist, and France would have converted to Islam sometime after that battle.

From the crowning of Charlemagne as Emperor of the Romans on December 25, 800 CE to the beginning of the Protestant Reformation in the 16th century, the only acceptable religion within the West was Roman Catholicism. While Roman Catholicism was nominally affiliated with Eastern Orthodox Christianity, that came to an end in 1054 CE, and from that point, the two societies went their separate ways. The east became the Byzantine Empire and Rome led Western Europe into Western Civilization. The Ottoman Empire conquered the Byzantine Empire in 1453, allowing the West to claim supreme control upon the defeat of the Ottoman Empire during World War I.

To summarize, every society has a founding religion, and Roman Catholicism was the accidentally chosen religion used for the founding of Western society. Modern Christianity means anything you want it to mean. Somewhere among the thousands of sects of Christianity you can find just about any idea important to you as an idea within that sect of Christianity. As an atheist and agnostic, I've always favored Unitarian-Universalism, which many Christians deny is even Christian.[23] Such are the disputes among religionists.

---

[22] The Battle of Tours (or the Battle of Poitiers for the Franks; also, the Battle of the Highway of the Martyrs for the Umayyad Caliphate) took place on 10 October 732 at a location between Tours and Poitiers in France. The Franks had a slightly smaller army, but they inflicted far greater casualties, due to the better leadership and strategies on the Frankish side.

[23] Agnosticism is an epistemological stance. Atheism is a metaphysical stance. These will be explained later.

But there is no denying that secularism has been on the rise for the past few decades as people recognize the corruption inherent in many sects of Christianity. Yes, there are many Christians who do good. But there seem to be many Christians who do bad things. I will not enumerate the good and the bad. But I will claim that Christianity can't be the religion associated with our new society. It has a bad reputation among many other populations due to prior bad acts.

I am offering an alternative to Christianity that will motivate people towards generosity towards other people in need, not just generosity towards church buildings and staff. We want food banks and housing for the homeless, not a larger auditorium with better entertainment to draw in more money during each church service.

Many people see the United States and other nations each moving towards an authoritarian system, each nation moving at its own pace and in its own way. We are headed towards a government of tyranny. Spengler predicted "gradually increasing crudity and despotism." Each of us must decide upon a strategy for survival during this transition phase. While others offer advice for survival within the context of Western Civilization, I'm offering an alternative that involves jettisoning Western Civilization in favor of something better.

Professor Timothy Snyder offers us a recipe in his book *On Tyranny: Twenty lessons from the Twentieth Century*.[24] If you choose the former path of sticking within the paradigm of Western Civilization, Snyder's book becomes essential advice for retaining as much of yourself as will be possible as authoritarianism advances. If you choose the path I recommend in Part II of this book, Snyder's book becomes essential grounding for dealing with the outside world while we grow the movement that will hopefully be able to create a peaceful takeover before the authoritarians make that impossible.

We should never forget some authoritarian governments did temporarily end at the time of the fall of the Soviet Union. We must be ready for any similar event towards the end of the current authoritarian

---

[24] See https://timothysnyder.org/on-tyranny for more.

11

interval. The more nations where we can create welcoming communities of our members, the more opportunities will exist for our members to escape from the "worst of the worst" nations around the world. In my estimation, the second tier of worst nations as I write this begins with China, but there is a steady stream of migrants out of China, as China seeks to have its citizens obtain outside educational experiences. And many of those people, once exposed to outside education, choose to make their homes outside of China. The first tier of worst nations includes North Korea, Afghanistan, and Iran, but even there a small number of people manage to escape each year. So long as some places are better to be than others, and so long as the ability to travel exists, there will be a flow of people from worse places to better places. It has always been so.

Also, keeping silent is an assist to the authoritarians, and silence makes silent people complicit in the atrocities committed by the authoritarians. We should remember this famous lesson from World War II:

First, they came for the socialists, and I did not speak out—
because I was not a socialist.
Then they came for the trade unionists, and I did not speak out—
because I was not a trade unionist.
Then they came for the Jews, and I did not speak out—
because I was not a Jew.
Then they came for me—and there was no one left to speak for me.

—Martin Niemöller[25]

Niemöller was a prominent Lutheran pastor in the 1920s and 1930s. But he came out against Hitler's interference in the church beginning

---

[25] This is the version of his words displayed on the walls of the United States Holocaust Museum, as re-ported on its website, located at. https://encyclopedia.ushmm.org/content/en/article/martin-niemoeller-first-they-came-for-the-socialists .

in 1933, and he was sent to a series of prisons and camps beginning in 1937. After the end of the war, Niemöller would frequently give impromptu speeches where he would express sentiments like those written above. He did not always say things the same way, but he always expressed a similar thought: If you see something that is wrong, say that it is wrong, and do what you can to make it right.

While most of the members of the organizations which I propose to form in Part II will live openly within societies willing to at least tolerate us, some of those members must live under deep cover, able to slip in and out of threatening situations as needed to keep hope alive among other members stuck within harsh systems of oppression.[26]

Another point which we must keep in mind is that "we must all hang together, or assuredly we shall all hang separately."[27] To succeed, we must never "rat out" our fellow members. There are many examples of how to continue a tolerable existence within an intolerable system. And ratting out your fellow members is not a method of success.

Finally, we return to the joint topic of religion and philosophy before I end this introduction. Any religion is just a pre-packaged philosophy. If a religion is well thought out, it has all the elements of a philosophy. Part I of this book explains this and sets forth the idea of an atheistic philosophy which I propose to adopt as the religion of our new society.

If you consider yourself a devout Christian or a devout follower of some other religion, I will still welcome you to our small society of Good People so long as you are a good person and agree to follow our moral principles, which are not antagonistic to any religious beliefs.[28] I only ask that you educate your children outside of faith-based schools and allow them each to choose for themselves what beliefs to hold onto. Once the accidental nature of our various religious systems is understood, it should be easier to pick a philosophy (religion) which is based upon a firmer footing of "**REALITY**."

---

[26] An example of such a thing would be contacting Uyghurs in China. An elaborate cover would be required to even obtain permission from China to visit the region.

[27] Quote attributed to Benjamin Franklin at the signing of the Declaration of Independence on July 4, 1776. This quote may have been originated by someone else, according to a Franklin scholar.

[28] But we do strongly believe in the right of self-defense against any attack.

Part II takes that philosophy and sets forth a plan for building a virtual society that can eventually become a real society if enough people join us. And that is why I am writing this book. Let's join ourselves together and get out of this "Imperium of gradually increasing crudity and despotism." We don't want to live in such an Imperium. Nobody should want that. So, let's put that Imperium into the trash heap of history and invent something a lot better. **JOIN ME!!**

To get things going, I've set up an online presence using my Agnostic Church domain name. Please join here:

https://www.agnostic.org/

PART I

THE PHILOSOPHY OF REALITY

ENLIGHTENMENT FOR THE UNENLIGHTENED

(THIS PAGE IS INTENTIONALLY BLANK)

PART I
INTRODUCTION

A new civilized society necessarily begins with a new "religion." In this case, I'm proposing to adopt a philosophy as a religion. If you look deeply at the question, any religion is merely a pre-packaged philosophy. So, it will be interesting to see what develops from this choice to call it a philosophy, like Confucianism, rather than a god-guided religion. We have no god(s).

In past centuries, it would have been inconceivable for an educated person to have no grounding in philosophy. Many of the reading assignments for anything beyond grammar school would have been drawn from ancient philosophers like Aristotle, Plato, and Socrates. And to this day, most advanced degrees issued by major universities are Doctor of Philosophy (PhD) degrees. At the highest levels of education philosophy is required knowledge.

But while modern public education has been a great foundation for the advancement of our economy, along the way the foundations of education were discarded. Among the discards were any real grounding in philosophy beyond an occasional mention about texts from the ancient Greeks. Most people learn nothing of the major topic areas of philosophy or the major principles which guide philosophical investigation.

Part of the problem is that philosophy itself has become largely incomprehensible. We can still read the great conclusive systems of Greek philosophy with translations from Aristotle and Plato. But the great conclusive systems of Western Civilization by writers such as Goethe, Hegel, and Kant are largely incomprehensible to even trained readers. Modern philosophers like Wittgenstein spend most of their time arguing over language and meaning, with the extreme post-modern view of subjectivism claiming to negate the idea that there can ever be valid communication between two people, thus negating the value of any communication of any philosophical ideas.

17

My own view is that the failures of these philosophers to be widely understood are rooted in their attempts to drive towards a particular final thesis (which is almost never accepted by any other philosophers) rather than create a teaching document for students to comprehend.

Western Civilization grew out of the Western Roman Empire which, in turn, adopted almost completely the philosophical writings of the ancient Greeks who preceded them. The monks who preserved books by copying them over and over during the centuries before the invention of the printing press and modern "survivable" paper also largely picked the texts of the great Greek writers for preservation. While some basic ideas in those ancient texts from 24 centuries ago are still valid, it is questionable whether what philosophers in a Greek city-state could say about modern politics. The German historian and philosopher Oswald Spengler pointed out that the Greek conceptions of reality were very different than what we know today.

Philosophy is a personal endeavor in a particular time and place. The great schools of philosophy usually consist of one great writer and a few followers who flesh out the ideas of the "great one." To this day, there has not been any philosophy which transcends the time, place, and author of the original version.

Part of the reason for the above is the fact that each great philosopher was striving for a grand conclusive vision which was their personal view at their own time and place. No attempt was made to address the needs of an average person with an average education. My main goal is to simplify philosophy to the point that such a person can have a useful introduction to philosophy without much confusion, which results in many side trips to address exceptions to rules and so forth.

The one philosophy course I took in the first year of college was extremely confusing because it attempted to present ideas from a dozen major philosophers, all of whom had ideas which conflicted with one another. This will not work well for a simplified overview text. My hope for this section is to present some ideas which are timeless and not rooted in some place. And I intend to keep this section as short as possible.

The word "philosophy" comes from the ancient Greek words for "love" (**philos**) and "wisdom" (**sophia**). It has long been presumed that the wise person will survive better than an unwise person. Thus, to love life is to love wisdom and the love of life and wisdom leads to survival of the individual, group, nation, species, and eventually of all living things. This hierarchy of survival is the foundation of ethics, as will be discussed in a later chapter.

There has been a long disagreement over what areas are covered by philosophy. Different philosophers include or exclude different topics for various reasons. My own view is that philosophy provides the infrastructure and connective tissue for all knowledge, and thus all topics are embraced by philosophy to one degree or another. This kind of thinking leads to the fact that almost all advanced degrees are styled as Doctor of Philosophy (PhD) degrees.

The main concept of philosophy is "rational inquiry," mostly using a system of Logic, which itself is usually a part of a complete philosophy. Logic is then used to investigate the other three basic topics of philosophy, which are described by Ayn Rand's three questions:[29]

1. **Where am I?** (Traditionally called "*Metaphysics*" but I call it "*Reality*")
2. **How do I know this?** (Traditionally called "*Epistemology*")
3. **What do I do next?** (Traditionally called "*Ethics*")

Different philosophers may set forth a different set of questions. For instance, Kant specifies four questions, "What can I know?", "What should I do?", "What may I hope?" and "What is a human being?". Apart from "What should I do?" (Ethics), and "What can I know?" (Epistemology), his other two questions do not easily map into the traditional topic areas of philosophy. I chose to use Ayn Rand's three questions as my jumping off point for further discussion in part because Rand's ideas do map out that way, and they are explained in a very accessible short essay.

---

[29] The three questions come from the lead essay, with the same title, which is reprinted in her posthumous 1982 book *Philosophy: Who Needs It*. See https://en.wikipedia.org/wiki/Philosophy:_Who_Needs_It for more.

However, it should always be remembered that if it is actual knowledge, it always connects to philosophy in some way. Fiction and entertainment do not necessarily connect in that way, largely because the knowledge in such presentations is mostly made up.

The word "*Metaphysics*" is a coined word, made up by a later editor of the works of Aristotle. One definition of meta is "*after*" so Metaphysics means, in this sense, "*after physics.*" The editor used the word to describe the writings of Aristotle, which were in the volumes presented in order by that editor after his books on physics (the physical, observable, and measurable universe).

Those books, and a huge quantity of later writings by other authors which bring out similar concepts, all deal with topics which are not subject to physical measurement. You can't settle questions on the nature of God by physically measuring God.[30]

Many topics normally dealt with in metaphysical writings deal with questions of logic and meaning. We need logic as a tool to look at concepts within human knowledge. Without logic we cannot sort concepts into categories such as "true" or "false." For this reason, logic becomes a foundation for the philosophical topic of Epistemology, which is represented by Rand's second question: *How do I know this?*[31] I might have an opinion on some topic, but is that opinion justified by facts and logic? Epistemology sets forth the principles which guide us to make such decisions.

In grade school, logic is usually taught as part of mathematics. This divorces logic from philosophy, which is a horrible omission in the teaching of young people. But it has a political purpose: thou shalt not question religion, and thou shalt not use logic to look at religious ideas.

Unfortunately, this ancient split between physics and metaphysics imports a bias towards dualism into philosophical discussions.

---

[30] Most distinct religious communities can't even agree as to the definition of the word "God." For Christians, "God" is the triune God of Christianity, Father, Son, and Holy Spirit. Jews and Muslims each recognize a singular distinct God. Hindus and other ancient religions have huge pantheons of gods. Buddhism doesn't have gods per se, but it does recognize eternally enlightened ones who are worshiped for their enlightenment.

[31] Or maybe Kant's question: "What can I know?"

"Aristotle worried that a material organ [the brain] could not have the range and flexibility that are required for human thought."[32] Modern philosophers and scientists would challenge this assertion by Aristotle. As we are increasingly able to measure brain activity in detail, the old views of Aristotle have proven wrong.[33] Aristotle advocated for mind and body dualism, which in a religious context becomes body and soul dualism. To understand these things is to understand the quicksand upon which Christianity is constructed.

Is the mind distinct from the body (in a dualism sense)? Or is the mind an emergent property of a physical brain?[34] We don't need to limit our investigations to just human beings. We can observe mental activities in many lower animals, and this makes it much easier to argue in favor of a non-dualistic answer.

Scientific investigation has come a long way since Aristotle's books on physics. Philosophers of science have systemized scientific investigation into a body of writings which document modern "scientific method." Scientific methods produce most of the value which we see in a modern economy. A business will waste resources if it pursues false things, particularly if it is already known that they are false.[35] Wasting resources is bad for the bottom line of any business, so most businesses will rely upon scientific findings to create valuable products to sell in the marketplace (or economy).

The overarching principle is this: if you want to know the truth, use scientific methods to discover the truth. Religion argues in favor of an unverifiable "revealed truth" which must be taken on faith. Religion indeed adds value to a society, which is why every known civilization included a "main religion" as part of its existence. Our own Western

---

[32] Stanford Encyclopedia of Philosophy online, *Dualism*, section 4.6, viewed December 15, 2024, at https://plato.stanford.edu/entries/dualism/ (which see).

[33] See, for example, *Consciousness Explained* by Daniel C. Dennett (1991). This is not an assertion that the debate is settled. But there are now physical measurements for philosophers to argue over.

[34] Stanford Encyclopedia of Philosophy online, *Emergent Properties*, viewed December 15, 2024, at https://plato.stanford.edu/entries/properties-emergent/ (which see).

[35] Unless, of course, it is an enterprise engaging in fraud for profit.

Civilization was founded with Roman Catholic Christianity as the sole religion.[36]

The Byzantine Civilization was founded with Eastern Orthodox Christianity as the sole religion. And the Arab Civilization was founded on one set of beliefs, but converted to Islam after Mohammed experienced a religious conversion which he then propagated as a conquering movement. But value and success do not necessarily translate into the truth. To have truth you must survive analysis in the light of facts and logic. Thomas Henry Huxley claimed in its simplest form:

> *... that it is wrong for a man to say that he is certain of the objective truth of any proposition unless he can produce evidence which logically justifies that certainty.*[37]

Evidence and logical justification are the foundations of scientific methods and they are thus the foundations for any claim of truth. This answers the second question: "How do we know?"

The third question is "What do we do next?" This is a question about the philosophical subject of ethics. Ethical principles should guide our path forward in all aspects of our lives. A simple ethical principle is "Do as you would be done by."[38] While that is a good principle, it is not sufficient for a complete ethical system. It presumes that individuals already know what is good, and that each person wishes to be treated well by others and thus is instructed to treat others according to the good principles that they themselves desire.

Once the three questions are properly dealt with, we can then look at religion and see it as a valuable aspect of civilized society, but not as a source of "truth" (whatever that means). And Part II of this book builds upon the final question of "What do we do next?" Western

---

[36] Arguably, Western Civilization (or Society) was founded on December 25, 800 CE, when Charlemagne was crowned Emperor of the Romans by the Roman Catholic Pope in Rome.

[37] Huxley, Thomas, *Agnosticism and Christianity* (1889), essay originally published in the magazine *Nineteenth Century* in May of 1889.

[38] This is the so-called Golden Rule, which is phrased in many ways. See https://en.wikipedia.org/wiki/Golden_Rule for more.

Civilization is in its "Decline and Fall" phase.[39] Since there are no barbarian tribes "outside" of The West to storm in and terminate Western Civilization, the change to something new must come from within. Part II presents a proposal for what to do next.

---

[39] A reference to the book by Edward Gibbon, The History of the Decline and Fall of the Roman Empire (1776-1789), but with respect to modern Western Civilization instead of to the Roman Empire.

(THIS PAGE IS INTENTIONALLY BLANK)

CHAPTER 1
SOME HISTORICAL PERSPECTIVES

The United States, where I live, exists as part of Western Civilization. That is named after the former Western Roman Empire, where Rome was the capital. The Byzantine Empire was the corresponding civilization for the Eastern Roman Empire. The Byzantines separated themselves from Rome in 330 CE, long before Rome fell.

All civilizations begin with a combination of a ruling aristocracy and a religious movement. For Western Civilization, the ruling aristocracy came from the former Roman province of Gaul. Upon the fall of Rome, the Merovingian dynasty began to assert control over Gaul. Because Rome had fallen under control of the Christian religion circa 300 CE, Gaul was well populated with Christian clerics at the beginning of the Merovingian dynasty. In 751 CE, Pepin III the Short completed a successful coup d'état against the Merovingians by having himself elected as King of Francia by the Frankish nobles. His elder son, Charles I The Great (known as Charlemagne) largely founded what we now know as Western Civilization by persuading the Pope in Rome to crown him Emperor of the Romans in 800 CE. Later rulers were known as the Holy Roman Emperor, a title which existed and was held by his descendants until that monarchy was abolished in 1806. The Roman Catholic religion was the official religion of the Holy Roman Empire throughout its existence. The Protestant Reformation had some effect around the edges of the Empire, helped along by the greed of kings like Henry VIII of England, but the Protestant faith is still essentially Christian, so its adoption anywhere did not separate that area from Western Civilization.

If you probe far enough back in time into human history, you reach a point where there is a truly socialist economy. A small tribe of humans, mostly related to each other, ekes out a living through farming, hunting, and gathering. In such a primitive environment, all property is held in common, and the goal of the socialist utopia, *"from each according to his ability to each according to his need,*" is naturally realized in such a primitive setting.

Over time, a monarchy develops, and as bands of warriors conquer adjacent lands, the monarch becomes wealthy and appropriates all property rights for their own benefit. By the time you get to a person such as Julius Caesar, who conquered (and thus owned) the Roman province of Gaul, that conquest made Caesar fabulously wealthy. But I get ahead of myself.

Once a monarchy develops, the monarch needs several specific things, which require special skills to create, for instance, weapons of war. While an early blacksmith might create a sword, over time specialists in sword making arise to meet the need for even better weapons.

One of the competitions in which nations engage is the creation of better weapons of war. A wise ruler promotes the development of the skillsets needed to do better than any prospective enemy. As time goes by, a merchant class arises, and an economy starts to take shape. While the first estate (*nobility*) provides management, and the second estate (*religious leadership*) provides inspiration and moral cohesion, the third estate (*merchants*) provides the economy which supports the population's desire for more than just the necessities of life. The more things that people want the more merchants will attempt to supply those things at an acceptable price.

In this kind of early economy, a man's word was his bond, and no merchant would wish to become known as a cheater. This desire to maintain a good reputation is the source of modern libel laws. However, in our complex modern economy, individual (bad) reputation is easily disguised through corporate shells.

As the merchant class develops, many distinct specialties arise. The butcher, the baker, and the candlestick maker (from the childhood rhyme) are all examples of specialists. Educators are one of the specialists, and in Western Civilization, the better educators organize themselves into universities to teach or to write or to otherwise advance knowledge. Some universities become known as places for scientific research.[40] Gradually, education becomes big business. This is the path taken by Western Civilization down to the present day.

Oswald Spengler claimed that the end of the Holy Roman Empire in 1806 marked a great change for Western Civilization. It was the end of the "is Becoming" stage and the beginning of the "has Become" stage.[41] Once Western Civilization solidifies in that way, it naturally begins to decay (or "decline"). Having ditched the First Estate (monarchy) and downgraded the control mechanisms of the Second Estate (religion), the Third Estate (merchants) becomes the supreme rulers, no longer bound by the ethics of loyalty to monarchs or the church. Instead, ethics devolves into the constant seeking of greater and greater sums of money, and that is the antithesis of ethics.

Of course, the Roman Catholic Church had transformed itself into a vast business enterprise several centuries before 1806. In 1517 Martin Luther complained about the selling of indulgences by corrupt church leaders.[42] Before that, huge houses of worship were built with correspondingly huge sums of money raised to enable building. It can be argued that the corruption of capitalism is modeled upon the corruption of the church which came before the modern economy.

Modern religion cannot exist in its present form without a constant flow of money from the followers to pay for the facilities and staff for their chosen religious institutions. But the greater the focus is on collecting money, the more the religion becomes corrupted by that very process of seeking ever greater sums of cash. That is, essentially, what Luther was objecting to.

I am deeply connected to Western Civilization. The founder, Emperor Charlemagne, is my 37th great grandfather. If you have ancestors from Western Europe, it is more likely than not that you too are a

---

[40] The article List of research universities in the United States defines a set of criteria for recognizing a university as a "research university" and lists 146 such universities at the highest classification level as viewed on December 21, 2024.

[41] Spengler distinguished the "is Becoming" stage by labeling it as "Culture" and the "has become" stage by labeling it "Civilization." In normal usage, people just call it all "Civilization."

[42] See The indulgences controversy of Martin Luther from the online Encyclopedia Britannica, as viewed on December 21, 2024.

descendant of Charlemagne. The only difference is that I have a provable lineage back to him. Throughout time, monarchs and their subordinate rulers frequently engaged in extra-marital baby making. My lineage runs through *Isabella MacWilliam*, the illegitimate daughter of *King William I* of Scotland. The main question is whether the actual father acknowledges the child as his own. The more that DNA technology advances, the more difficult it becomes to conceal the true parentage and lineage of any person.[43]

Lord Acton wrote an observation (rule) about how power tends to corrupt.[44] That rule works just as well when referred to money. Money amounts to economic power, and it also corrupts if it is used to wield any kind of power over others. And yet, that is exactly what happens in modern business enterprises. I have heard business owners say things like "I follow the Golden Rule: He who has the gold makes the rules." In some sense, that is the essence of business ownership. But when business ownership becomes effectively ownership of the employees, that is a corrupt entity, and the employees are only a small amount better off than actual slaves.

The essential activity of modern business enterprises is the continuous seeking of ever greater profits. And that leads to a complete corruption of the moral value system which underlies business activities in the early days of the third estate. In those early days, the owner's reputation was on the line for every business interaction by anyone speaking on behalf of the business. Corporate structure separates ownership from management and insulates the reputations of owners (and, for that matter, most managers) for any misdeed committed by

---

[43] Current autosomal DNA technology can only make valid connections back approximately 250 years. But Whole Genome Sequencing (WGS), if applied using the same techniques as are currently used for the male Y chromosome, can very likely link lineages back to the beginning of the human species, or even before then. The main barriers to using WGS in this way is the size of the databases and the cost of the processing.

[44] John Dalberg-Acton, 1st Baron Acton, famously wrote: "Power tends to corrupt, and absolute power corrupts absolutely." Acton was noting the ill effects on human freedom the greater are the concentrations of power in society. The same can be said for concentrations of wealth, as we are now witnessing with Elon Musk. Musk's wealth is being translated into political power and used to hurt masses of people though influencing laws passed by Congress and actions of President Trump's government.

someone acting on behalf of the corporation. The larger the corporation is, the more economic power it has. And a few huge corporations have the power to take over the lives of "customers" (I wonder if "customer" is even the proper word to use for a relationship which is so controlling). Certainly, Apple, Google, and Microsoft exercise huge control over each of their customers by controlling the relationship between their customers and the rest of the Internet.[45] The goal for any corporation seeking maximum profits is to exercise monopoly control over a substantial market. Apple is the most successful at doing that, with Microsoft and Google still competing closely behind Apple. And while most consumers would say that they are happy with their choices, none of them are particularly free to change to a different service provider. And most consumers have no real idea of just how their service provider of choice is monetizing the relationship.

The era of the third estate begins with what purports to be political democracy. However, even at the beginning, it is democracy subordinate to economic power. In the early days of the United States, you needed to be a landowner to have the right to vote in democratic elections. England had similar restrictions upon voting rights centuries earlier when it began its system of parliamentary elections. So-called "direct democracy" (where people vote directly on the matters usually considered by a legislative body) exists only at the most local of levels (i.e., town councils). The usual situation is some form of representative democracy, where people elect representatives to vote on their behalf. Such a system is easily corrupted when money is used to influence the legislators. A vote is just another commodity.

As noted above, I am deeply and personally connected to Western Civilization. The founder, Emperor Charlemagne, is my 37th great grandfather. But the connection of Christianity to Western Civilization was made two generations earlier, by Charlemagne's grandfather,

---

[45] Apple is the most controlling of these three. It has a very successful phone, and that draws consumers into using Apple desktop and laptop computers, all of which run Apple software almost exclusively. Microsoft failed to establish itself in the phone market, and Google's Chrome operating system never gained much of an ecosystem of 3rd-party software. So, Microsoft and Google never were able to enforce the total ecosystem approach that has made Apple so successful.

Charles Martel. On October 10, 732 CE Martel led a Christian army of Franks against a larger Muslim army of the Umayyad Caliphate.[46] If Martel had lost, the Muslim army would likely have continued marching north to take Paris, and the Frankish kingdom would have become a province of the Umayyad Caliphate. There would not have been a Western Civilization, and Christianity would not have been the predominant religion of Western Europe. But for the outcome of that one battle on that single day, subsequent history would have been very different. And the entire Western Hemisphere would likely have been predominately Islamic rather than predominately Christian.

Since human lifetimes are so short, people tend to not have a good view of the sweep of a civilization over 10 to 20 centuries. People somehow believe that "progress" always moves humanity in a "forward" direction. However, civilization is more of a cyclical phenomenon than it is always "progress" in some direction or another. Oswald Spengler asserted that Western Civilization reached its peak and began its decline at about the time (in 1806) when the Holy Roman Empire was abolished. Over a century ago, Spengler wrote about the future Decline of the West (the title of his 2-volume book), predicting in broad brush strokes the path that Western Civilization has followed ever since.[47] The rise of nationalistic and authoritarian rule is part of what Spengler predicted for the time when democratic rule was coming to an end, and that is exactly what we are experiencing in the third decade of the 21st century. This is happening in parallel within many nations which are enmeshed within Western Civilization. Hungary is further along than Germany, but you can see the movement towards authoritarian rule in most nations that are part of "the West", and even many which are late joiners of "the West," such as India.

If humanity is to survive in a civilized form for another 1,000 years or more, we will need a new civilization for humans to join. Western

---

[46] See https://en.wikipedia.org/wiki/Battle_of_Tours for the Battle of Tours, also called the Battle of Poitiers by some Western sources, and called the Battle of the Highway of the Martyrs by Islamic historians.

[47] Other historians, such as Arnold Toynbee and Will Durant (with his wife, Ariel Durant) have made similar observations.

Civilization died over two centuries ago, and it continues strictly based on cultural inertia. Human happiness requires us to take a different path than the "formation of Caesarism"; "victory of force-politics over money"; "increasing primitiveness of political forms"; and "inward decline of the nations into a formless population, and constitution thereof as an Imperium of gradually increasing crudity and despotism," which is the path predicted by Spengler. To achieve happiness, we must embrace the wisdom of the ages, which is what my proposed philosophy offers to us. **This is the way.**[48]

---

[48] Yes, I did watch The Mandalorian. See Further Reading, which references an article on Mandalorian Philosophy. Sometimes, even fictional settings can be brought back to discussions of philosophy.

(THIS PAGE IS INTENTIONALLY BLANK)

CHAPTER 2
LOGIC

An understanding of logic is a prerequisite for understanding philosophy. Philosophy, in turn, must be grounded in a set of facts and supported by logical reasoning to some conclusion. You need both facts and logic to have any kind of rational thought. Unfortunately, the modern education system is designed to teach logic as a branch of mathematics and not as an introduction to philosophy. The idea is that students should not be taught how to evaluate the overall system within which they are being raised. If that were allowed, the students might discover the flawed foundation of their current social order. Thus, education is designed to deprive students of the basic tools for performing such an evaluation.

Mathematical logic is taught as if every problem has an exactly computable answer. However, only the simplest problems fall into this category. Most problems have solutions which are conditioned by some statement of probability. And in most cases, the probability isn't even stated openly. But the wise person will be aware that nothing in the real world involves an answer with complete certainty. This idea comes from the writings of David Hume (1711-1776), which are discussed below.[49] And Gödel's incompleteness theorems only add to the uncertainty which Hume raises. Wikipedia says this about Gödel's findings:

> *The first incompleteness theorem states that no consistent system of axioms whose theorems can be listed by an effective procedure (i.e. an algorithm) is capable of proving all truths about the arithmetic of natural numbers. For any such consistent formal system, there will always be statements about natural numbers that are true, but that are unprovable within the system.*

---

[49] See https://en.wikipedia.org/wiki/David_Hume for more on Hume.

The second incompleteness theorem, an extension of the first,
shows that the system cannot demonstrate its consistency.[50]

Thus, the reality of known logic and mathematics is such that we cannot obtain any conclusions with absolute certainty. We might say that in the past X has always led to, or caused, Y to happen. But that cannot operate as a guarantee that Y will always follow X because of causation. Proving causation is much more complicated than merely showing a relationship in time between two events. The famous quote is that "correlation does not imply causation."[51] Proving causation implies that a study of the mechanism(s) of causation is completed with the researcher(s) gaining a sufficient understanding of said mechanism(s) to thus prove that the result always proceeds from the actual cause. Correlation may cause such research to happen, but it will never be conclusive without such follow-on research.

As we shall see in a future chapter, the philosophy of reality is grounded in empiricism, which will include such studies of correlation and causation, and Hume claimed that empiricism could never produce a completely true and accurate depiction of reality. However, the tremendous successes of science over the past three centuries demonstrate that complete certainty is not a requirement for valuable results. We should proceed as if we are completely certain in the conclusions of science, but, as it is for science itself, ready to detect any low-probability exception and deal with it appropriately when detected.

This probability approach works retrospectively as well as prospectively, and it works best with a team of cooperating researchers who have a widely varied set of personal experiences. Historians evaluate writings about historical events using a combination of probabilities and other techniques to come up with a probability of the accuracy and

---

[50] This quotation is from https://en.wikipedia.org/wiki/G%C3%B6del%27s_incompleteness_theorems as viewed on 1 Jan 2025.

[51] See https://en.wikipedia.org/wiki/Correlation_does_not_imply_causation for a lengthy discussion of this point.

completeness of some historical report of an event.[52] And teams of historians reach better conclusions than does a single individual.

All this leads to the following two conclusions:

First, we can proceed as if we have complete certainty in our results so long as the results meet the high standards for scientific conclusions.

Second, we must not let the lack of complete certainty provide a wedge point for the introduction of completely unjustified alternative conclusions.

This second point is important when we discuss competing religions. For instance, the advocates for Christianity will arrive claiming complete certainty (in their minds) for the truth of the Christian religion. The fact that my religious views allow for a lack of certainty does not mean that my religion is less correct than Christianity. On the contrary, such a religion is a more accurate reflection of reality than is the Christian religion.[53] And each conclusion must stand or fall on its own merits. Let the advocates for Christianity prove its truth. Logic is a very difficult topic. One of the reasons it is so difficult is that logic has been debated for thousands of years, and written records exist of numerous fallacies used in arguments over those many years.[54] An argument seeking truth will be less likely to contain fallacies while an argument seeking to convince an audience will be more likely to contain fallacies.

In other words, the more polemical the argument, the more likely it is to contain numerous fallacies. But again, this is mere probability, not certainty.

---

[52] Always remembering that in general, the winners write the histories. If available, it is always useful to compare the history written by both the winners and the losers. Unfortunately, there are few historical events where both sides created substantial histories of some given confrontation.

[53] The Christian religion is believed by less than half of the people in the world. However, even if everyone in the world believes in Christianity, that would not justify anyone changing their view to believe in Christianity. That is a logically fallacious argument, as we shall see shortly.

[54] See the Wikipedia list of fallacies: https://en.wikipedia.org/wiki/List_of_fallacies as an example. The list, while very long, is by no means exhaustive.

Some of the more common fallacies include:

- Ad hominem – an attack on the person rather than the argument.[55]

- Argument from authority – a claim that a person of high station or a given expertise supports the argument, therefore it must be true.[56]

- Argumentum ad populum – a claim based upon the number of supporters.[57]

- Argument from incredulity – a claim that it can't be imagined that the assertion being evaluated can't be true (or not true).[58]

- Begging the question or assuming the conclusion – a claim that asserts the conclusion (in some form or in some part) as part of the premises of the assertion.[59]

- Equivocation – the use of a term with a hidden set of meanings which are not distinguished properly.[60]

The above list is merely a sample of known species of logical fallacies. It is very difficult to construct a logically valid argument to some conclusion. And the powerful people in society fear that the knowledge of valid argumentation would lead to the population abandoning their current leadership, so they generally suppress education about rhetorical logic. If it is presented at all in the grade school curriculum, it will be in the form of a class on debate. Few will take such a class because it is perceived as generally worthless to a person's life, unless they

---

[55] See https://en.wikipedia.org/wiki/Ad_hominem for more.

[56] See https://en.wikipedia.org/wiki/Argument_from_authority. For instance, the Pope claims to write infallible truth in certain circumstances. See https://en.wikipedia.org/wiki/Papal_infallibility for more. One version of this allows people to vote on what is true. But you can't vote that Pi equals exactly 3. Math says that is false.

[57] See https://en.wikipedia.org/wiki/Argumentum_ad_populum for more. The counter argument is that if everyone believes an erroneous belief, it is still an erroneous belief. That is the reality.

[58] See https://en.wikipedia.org/wiki/Argument_from_incredulity for more.

[59] See https://en.wikipedia.org/wiki/Begging_the_question for more.

[60] See https://en.wikipedia.org/wiki/Equivocation for more.

choose to be a politician. Who else makes a living through formal debate? **Nobody!**[61]

The inability to reach an exact and provable conclusion using logic has some consequences in our lives. One consequence is that it provides an opening for religious zealots to arrive while claiming that their religion is grounded upon absolute certainty. But it is the absolute certainty of a fictional universe, supported solely by their own strong beliefs in the accumulated fictions. Weak minded average (or below average) people will be easily deluded because absolute certainty is a far more desirable emotional state than the eternal uncertainty which accompanies knowing the truth (or "Reality"). Such certainty provides a basis for a strong leader to motivate citizens to "die for their country" (which helps the leader, but not the people who die). This is one reason that every known civilization begins with a religion, which the leader uses to discipline the citizens to act as the leader wishes. But if you love the truth, you must learn to accept and live with the actual uncertainty which "the truth" entails. **Can you handle the truth?**[62]

Trained scientists are exactly the people whose occupation necessarily seeks truth and thus they must live with uncertainty. But the uncertainty is bound by scientific knowledge. I know that there is a longshot possibility that a sinkhole might open and swallow my house. But I cannot live in fear of that possibility. If I have some reason to worry, I can hire an expert to conduct a scientific study. But in most cases, there is no reason to worry, so spending that money isn't a worthwhile expenditure.

---

[61] In the 19th century English speaking world, there were men who made substantial living giving paid lectures, some of which would be in the form of a formal debate. Some of that persisted into the 20th century, but the Internet largely killed such debates by the early 21st century. By the time I am writing this, debate happens mostly in the form of segments on television news and in podcasts, neither of which are constrained by the rules of formal debating. Many television and podcast hosts are major media stars who do make millions of dollars, but they make money by drawing an audience with provocative content, not by hosting and scoring a formal debate. Even debates by candidates for President of the United States would seem to be a dying art form. After the debacles during the 2024 election cycle, including the total avoidance of the Commission on Presidential Debates, it remains to be seen if the tradition will continue for future election cycles.

[62] A reference to the famous line from the movie A Few Good Men, where Jack Nicholson screams "You can't handle the truth!"

Scientists are trained to accept (and document) failure as a natural part of scientific research. In most cases, well documented failures are almost as valuable as well documented successes. The key question is whether the documented case study provides insight into the underlying logic of how the universe operates.

And we must not forget that working in teams produces better results than everyone working as disconnected individuals. Certainly, one individual might have a brilliant insight into some aspects of a problem. Einstein's Theories of Relativity are an example of this.[63] But it has taken a century of experimentation by numerous research teams to validate Einstein's conclusions. Einstein provided a brilliant idea. But applying it to the real world took teamwork across many decades by numerous research teams each working on some aspects of Einstein's ideas.

If someone is trying to sell you some certainty, then you should know they are trying to sell you a lie. True certainty is an impossibility. But our modern advertising culture tries to warp our brains to accept incredible claims as pure truth. We should evaluate such claims the same way we would if we were watching an infomercial on television. The essence of advertising is to over promise and under deliver, which is the opposite of the good practices of a person-to-person business transaction. At the beginning of the merchant class in Western Civilization, reputation was everything, and a habit of under promising and over delivering added to your personal reputation over time.[64] In modern times, everything is labeled with marketing puffery to obscure the true reputation of the product. Fortunately, it is frequently possible to use modern technology to investigate the true reputation of any given product. However, even then we must beware of false online reviews of both positive and negative natures. It is hard to know what to believe within the web of deceit created by modern advertising. But logic provides a path out of the morass, if we learn how to employ it properly.

---

[63] There are two theories. See https://en.wikipedia.org/wiki/Theory_of_relativity for more.

[64] The so-called "baker's dozen," 13 items instead of 12, is an example of over delivering. That isn't seen in the modern era.

Training people in the basics of logic should be an objective of a modern education. The fact that it is not taught is a shame, which causes our society to take the wrong path to perdition.[65] People ignorant of logic are more easily defrauded, and the business interests which control our society wish to perpetrate fraud upon consumers at a much lower cost. So, they do what they can to ensure that people remain ignorant of concepts which would help them survive in the face of businesses defrauding them. But that is a topic for a later chapter on the economy.

This chapter concludes that people ought to be trained in the basics of logical thought. And they ought to be trained to consider important questions in teams if they seek to find a closer approximation to the ultimate truth.[66]

---

[65] As I write this, the most recent failure of society was to vote Trump in as President of the United States.

[66] There are many ways to do this. Even the way a Quaker Meeting considers a controversy is one way of having a team approach to solving a problem with logical reasoning.

(THIS PAGE IS INTENTIONALLY BLANK)

CHAPTER 3
PHILOSOPHY

Everyone has a philosophy. But very few people think at all about what their philosophy is. This point was made by Ayn Rand in her lecture and essay *Philosophy, Who Needs It?*[67] Very few average people receive any education at all in philosophy. This does not mean people don't learn philosophy. The other topics which a person learns from early childhood until graduation all bring along various elements of philosophical thinking.

The biggest part of a person's initial philosophy is the religion that (usually) parents impart to their children. Any significant religion contains teachings about all the usual philosophical subjects of metaphysics (the nature of reality), epistemology (this holy book is the ultimate source of truth), ethics (these are the rules to live by), and so forth.

And here lies the major reason why philosophy isn't usually taught below the college level. Religion doesn't like it when people evaluate their religion against other religions or systems of thinking. Philosophy does exactly that by asking each of us to think about the very nature of things like existence, knowledge, truth, and the rules for living. Religion asks us to focus only upon the teachings of that religion which a person has chosen to (or been told to) affiliate with. There are crass commercial reasons for this. Religion relies upon (usually) voluntary contributions of money to exist, and if you decide to affiliate with a different religion, that cash flow will be lost to the people benefiting from those contributions previously.

A family which leaves the Roman Catholic Church and affiliates with an evangelical Christian church moves an income stream away from the Catholic hierarchy and into the hierarchy of the evangelical church. Do you wonder why the evangelical church has a live band and lots of music during the service? It is because the increased value of entertainment increases the amount of money flowing into church

---

[67] See https://en.wikipedia.org/wiki/Philosophy:_Who_Needs_It for more. The essay is the lead essay in the book of the same name, published posthumously in 1982.

coffers. A so-called "megachurch" has a huge audience which then contributes a proportionally larger quantity of money towards the incomes of a staff which is only slightly larger than that of a traditional church. The pastors may say that they are worried about saving souls, but (with some exceptions) what they worry most about is the quantity of money which flows into their pocket.

If you are lucky enough to attend a university, if you look at the Department of Philosophy, you will frequently find professors whose specialty is Philosophy of Religion. Some people have been known to include "Religion" as one of the branches of philosophy. This view is wrong. Religions are more like individual species of philosophy rather than a topic area within philosophy, along with metaphysics, epistemology, or ethics. The philosophy of the Roman Catholic Church is better compared with the philosophy of Aristotle, Kant, or Wittgenstein. Each of these offers a particular view on each of the main topics of philosophy. And each of the many sects of Christianity or Islam or any other religion is simply a packaged philosophy with assertions about each (or at least most of each) philosophical topic we might choose to look at.

In 1895 the Founder and first President of Cornell University, the great educator Andrew Dickson White, published a lengthy book.[68] It had a similar theme to Part I of this book. The title was *The Warfare Of Science With Theology*.[69] In his introduction he writes:

> *I simply try to aid in letting the light of historical truth into that decaying mass of outworn thought which attaches the modern world to medieval conceptions of Christianity, and which still lingers among us — a most serious barrier to religion and morals, and a menace to the whole normal evolution of society.*

---

[68] See https://en.wikipedia.org/wiki/Andrew_Dickson_White for more.
[69] Read it at https://infidels.org/library/historical/the-warfare-of-science-with-theology/ (complete text).

Oswald Spengler would have understood that a philosophy formulated by Judeo-Christian thinkers of two millennia ago could not be made relevant to a modern world informed by scientific thinking. He developed one-word descriptions for each significant civilization. Western Civilization was Faustian. Classical civilization was Apollinian. The three great Abrahamic religions produced a Magian civilization. Each worldview is essentially incomprehensible to the other. Here we can view science as Faustian and (at least Christian) theology as Magian. Thus, the Magian worldview inherent in the Christian religion is greatly at odds with Western Culture and its Faustian worldview. This warfare cannot be resolved because the mindset of each side can't conceive of a middle ground. The philosophical foundations of each side utterly reject the premises and foundations of the other.

There have been attempts to force a compromise. One was advanced by the scientist Stephen Jay Gould.[70] He defined the concept of "Non-Overlapping Magisteria" (NOMA).[71] That concept tells science to stick to science and religion to stick to religion. The famous quote is:

> *"Science gets the age of rocks, and religion the rock of ages; science studies how the heavens go, religion how to go to heaven."[72] But these attempts at a truce always fail because both sides naturally seek power over the other and neither side is willing to "let well enough alone."*

Once we realize that science and religion are two competing philosophies, we will understand that the war will continue for as long as there are a substantial number of advocates on each side of their disagreements.

From the 1940s through the 1980s, the US Supreme Court embraced the idea that public schools ought not be used to indoctrinate children

---

[70] See https://en.wikipedia.org/wiki/Stephen_Jay_Gould for more.

[71] See https://en.wikipedia.org/wiki/Non-overlapping_magisteria for a discussion.

[72] Stephen Jay Gould, book, *Rock of Ages: Science and Religion in the Fullness of Life* .

on matters of religion. Subsequent decades have been spent gradually backsliding to allow various religious activities in or around school functions. This backsliding is possible because there is no clear line between what is prohibited by the so-called "Establishment Clause" of the First Amendment and its adjacent "Free Exercise Clause." Finding the proper balance has always been left to the "common sense" of the people, and "common sense" is increasingly uncommon. As I write this, the news is reporting that states like Texas and Oklahoma are trying to introduce what amounts to Christian Sunday School teachings into public grade school classes. This was banned by the Supreme Court back in the 1960s, but who knows what stance today's Supreme Court might take?

As we cycle through the decades of life, different topics become the subject of controversy. Charles Darwin published "*On the Origin of Species*" in 1859, and it created a firestorm after its release. Scientists defended it while religionists of many different types condemned it. The validity of Darwin's Theory of Evolution was debated, and it even fell out of favor in the decades between roughly 1880 and 1920. But eventually Darwin's ideas of *"natural selection"* survived scientific testing, while each alternative gradually fell by the wayside. By the time of the 1925 Scopes "monkey trial" science admitted that Darwin's theory of evolution by natural selection was the winner. Succeeding decades have not offered up any alternative.[73]

What later research accomplished was to illuminate the biological mechanisms of evolution, particularly genes encoded into DNA. Eventually, all forms of living organisms were shown to descend from the Last Universal Common Ancestor (LUCA).[74] Over billions of years,

---

[73] Lamarck's theory asserts that physical traits acquired during life, such as an athlete's muscles, could then be inherited by that person's offspring. It still refuses to completely die. We know that there are two components of inherited traits which we call Nature (based on DNA) and Nurture (how a child is raised). The mechanisms of inheritance are quite complex and don't actually fit within Lamarck's theory. DNA can provide a predisposition to grow muscles, but nurture is required to actually grow them. But because DNA is about half from each parent, there is no guarantee that one parent's DNA predisposition will be inherited by any given child of that parent. All of the possible nurture can't develop a trait where the DNA did not provide the underlying predisposition to a particular child.

[74] See https://en.wikipedia.org/wiki/Last_universal_common_ancestor for more.

every other living thing evolved using the process of descent with modification, from LUCA to every form of living thing today.

Today, the Roman Catholic Church is quite happy to assert that God created the evolutionary process and has guided that process towards the creation of humans. Thus, Catholic philosophy is compatible with scientific evolution. Unfortunately, not all Christian denominations are happy with that position. A subset of Protestant denominations who assert the literal truth of the (English!) words of the Bible denounce the whole idea of evolution, while claiming that God created every distinct species Himself through his own direct action.

The difficulty is that these two philosophies do not admit any common ground for ascertainment of The Truth. Science believes that truth is ascertained by scientific method while these religious denominations hold that the only truth comes from reading the literal words of the Bible.

This is the point at which someone who is intellectually interested in picking the correct answer must decide for themselves which philosophy is the proper one to pick. On the one hand, science has thousands of years of success to recommend it as the best philosophy. On the other hand, religion has even more thousands of years of competing religions that never once produced any new answers with the value of scientific discoveries. Almost by definition, religion is stuck with the exact words of a holy text, essentially inscribed into stone. Science, on the other hand, can change itself any time new facts arise which are incompatible with old assumptions.

While I have focused, by way of example, on the debate over evolution, almost all disputes between scientific philosophies and religious philosophies can be characterized in this same way. It is far easier for members of Western Civilization to consider the errors of ancient Egyptian religion than it is for those same people to consider the errors of Bible literalists over evolutionary science. Every religious believer disbelieves every other religion except their own. My philosophy only adds one extra religion to the pile of disbelief.[75]

And we should not forget that each religion is a packaged philosophy which each adherent is asked to believe as a matter of complete faith. Since most people are given their religious beliefs very early in life, usually by parents, the indoctrination is very easy, as young children have no intellectual defenses against such ideas. I was raised to be a Presbyterian because, from a young age, my mother took me to Sunday School at a nearby Presbyterian church. If my mother had been Roman Catholic, I doubtless would have been raised in the Catholic church. That is simply how religious beliefs are promulgated within a society.

And it doesn't matter what society we are discussing. Hindus in India teach their kids Hinduism. Buddhists in Thailand teach their kids Buddhism. Religion persists because parents indoctrinate their kids at an impressionable young age. And continuous reinforcement to and through adulthood keeps people attached to the religion of their own childhood.

Does science or religion have the better view? To ask the question that way is to make obvious the answer. Science has given us our modern lifestyle, with all its benefits. Religion desires to drag us back into the past, forgetting what science has taught us over recent centuries. Which is better? That is a personal and subjective judgment. I choose science. If I lived 600 years ago, the chances are good that I would be burned at the stake. Religion views me as a heretic or infidel, in part because I have developed my own personal philosophy that rejects other religions.

I choose science as the foundation of my philosophy, and the next few chapters will explore why. But first, let's bring back Ayn Rand to

---

[75] This thought is grounded in a quote from Stephen Roberts: "I contend that we are both atheists. I just believe in one fewer god than you do. When you understand why you dismiss all the other possible gods, you will understand why I dismiss yours."

set the stage. Rand asserts that the beginning of philosophy is to ask three questions without initially presuming the answers.

1. *Where are we?*
2. *How do we know?*
3. *What do we do next?*

Those three questions encompass the first three traditional topics of philosophy: Metaphysics (which I extend to "Reality"), Epistemology (or "Knowing"), and Ethics. There are three simple answers to these questions.

1. *Reality.*
2. *Science.*
3. *Survive.*

(THIS PAGE IS INTENTIONALLY BLANK)

CHAPTER 4
WHERE ARE WE? REALITY

The traditional first area of contemplation for philosophy is named Metaphysics, which means literally "after physics" (or sometimes "beyond physics").[76] The word comes from a description of the writings of the Greek philosopher Aristotle, and it means to distinguish foundational philosophical topics from physical sciences. The title was applied to a collection of writings assembled by later editors of Aristotle's essentially fragmentary works, by assembling discussions of physical sciences first and discussions of philosophical topics "after" physics. In other words, it simply referred to the relative position of the two sets of writings. Aristotle himself referred to the topic as "First Philosophy." That is a better description as it doesn't exclude discussions of physics from the overall topic.

The answer to Ayn Rand's first question is that we exist within the real world, or "reality" for short. Philip K. Dick had a pithy definition of reality:

> *"Reality is that which, when you stop believing in it, doesn't go away."[77]*

In other words, reality excludes any purely subjective perceptions of individuals. Reality doesn't care what anyone believes. Reality is not contingent upon any person existing at all, let alone that any person holds some belief about reality. Reality can be known, unknown or wrongly perceived by a human (or any other organism anywhere else within reality), but in any case, it is just as real.

Reality for most of us is an ordinary experience. We wake up in the morning, go through our day, and go to sleep at night. All the things we do involve existing within and interacting with reality. If we perceive something odd that happens, we might exclaim "was that real?" The

---

[76] See https://en.wikipedia.org/wiki/Metaphysics_(Aristotle) for details.
[77] Philip K. Dick, I Hope I Shall Arrive Soon.

answer could be yes or no, but either way we're asking if it is part of reality or not.

There are distinctions to be drawn between actual reality, perceived reality and imagined reality. Actual reality does not change regardless of what anyone thinks about it. Perceived reality may have varying degrees of difference between actual reality and what our senses perceive reality to be. Human senses have many known flaws, and our perceptions of reality may be thrown off by faulty senses or environmental tricks. For example, a *mirage* is known to be a trick played upon our eyes, or even a camera, by certain atmospheric conditions and our positioning vis-à-vis the purported location of the mirage.[78] An imagined reality is made up by a human mind. All works of fiction are versions of imagined reality, even if they incorporate some features of actual reality.

Most of what each of us knows about reality comes to us from stories told by other people and communicated in various ways. What I receive in such a case is the result of the combined efforts of several people. Perhaps there are multiple authors, editors, fact checkers, reviewers, etc. between the actual reality of what happened and the words or pictures which I receive in the form of a story about what happened. Even if there are photographs or videos in the story, it is a virtual certainty that the story does not exactly replicate the actual reality. But for the story to be useful to me, I don't need an exact recitation of the actual reality. I mostly just need the gist of the story to accurately reflect the actual reality.

It should be noted that we are in the first decades where it is increasingly easy to fabricate a false representation of reality.[79] A photograph used to be good evidence of the thing imaged in it. Of course, there are real situations where even a photograph with no modification or distortion still does not reflect actual reality (for instance, see the mention above of a mirage). There are known atmospheric conditions which can

---

[78] See https://en.wikipedia.org/wiki/Mirage for an explanation.

[79] It remains to be seen what the long-term impact will be of Artificial Intelligence. See https://en.wikipedia.org/wiki/Artificial_intelligence for more.

make a ship, which is sailing well over the horizon from the observer, appear to float in midair, and the vision is real because it can be photographed.[80] In this case, the image is completely real, but it does not accurately represent reality.

Almost since the beginning of photography, it has been possible for ingenious fraudsters to create believable photos which were utterly not real.[81] Special Effects for motion pictures exist to create just such misleading images. Unreal pictures add to the entertainment value of the presentation. Movie studios engage in research to develop new ways of creating such images to use in new movies, which they create. After more than a century of such development, the list of possible special effects is now very long. Examples include:

- Green screen photography,[82]
- Matte screen photography,[83]
- Motion capture suits,[84]
- Scale models presented as full-size objects,[85]
- Layering computer animations on top of photographed scenes.[86]

Various commercial enterprises earn money by transmitting stories. News companies compete to transmit the truth. Entertainment companies mostly transmit fiction (plus "real" entertainment like sporting events). Consumers pick and choose what is most suited to their own needs. The key is to properly inform the consumer, whether it is truth or fiction, which they are consuming. Failure to properly communicate

---

[80] The BBC reproduces one such photograph, and explains what happened, in an article from 2021, which can be read here: https://www.bbc.com/news/uk-england-cornwall-56286719

[81] One early example was the Cottingly Fairies where two young girls took pictures of themselves with a group of fairies. See: https://en.wikipedia.org/wiki/Cottingley_Fairies for more.

[82] This is very common, particularly when a normally earthbound object must be seen to fly. The flying cars in Mary Poppins and Back to the Future are two examples.

[83] This is a painting with a cut out area where the regular photography appears. The painting can give the illusion of a huge room when the actor is actually in a small space.

[84] Motion capture is a way of controlling animated characters to give them a more lifelike appearance.

[85] This is typically used when the object in question appears in a situation where there is no good size reference which would give away the fact it is a scale model. Filming a fleet of ships in a relatively small tank is one example.

[86] One of the best examples of this technique is the movie Who Framed Roger Rabbit.

this situation can lead to people taking unjustified actions in response to a fictional situation.[87]

One difficulty arises with news organizations when a reporter or even an entire news organization has a personal (or business) interest which overrides the usual motivation to present an accurate version of the truth. The reality behind the story is what it always is: actual reality. If the story is biased or untruthful more than is usual or normal, and if I expect accuracy, then I am being defrauded. When I detect such fraud, I should cease patronizing that news organization. In a modern media market, that would normally cause the news organization to lose income.

However, there are perverse situations where fraud is incentivized. If there is a large enough audience for a particular type of false story, then usual capitalist forces will incentivize some news organization to supply such false stories.[88] Political speech, and news reporting about political speech, are particularly vulnerable to reporting bias. Consumers of news should be somewhat skeptical of the stories which they read, and they should make themselves aware of the normal biases of whatever news media they consume.

One way to get closer to the real truth is to have a diversity of news sources, such as MSNBC, CNN, the New York Times, the Washington Post, the BBC, The Guardian, The Times of Israel, and Al Jazeera.[89] If

---

[87] Orson Wells had a spectacular situation with his radio broadcast of a version of The War of the Worlds by H. G. Wells. See https://en.wikipedia.org/wiki/The_War_of_the_Worlds_(1938_radio_drama) for more.

[88] If you want a specific example, I'm largely describing Fox News Network as disclosed by the settlement of Dominion Voting Systems v. Fox News Network. See https://en.wikipedia.org/wiki/Dominion_Voting_Systems_v._Fox_News_Network for more.

[89] This is my personal list of news organizations. I know MSNBC is biased to the left, but that's the way I lean, so I watch it the way Republicans watch Fox, which is biased to the right. CNN, the New York Times, and the Washington Post are so-called "mainstream" news outlets which generally adhere to traditional journalism ethics. I don't view them as biased for news, although each has a reputation to "lean left" to some degree. The Guardian is a left-leaning English newspaper and website. The BBC is owned by the UK government and is probably the least-biased news source on Earth. The Times of Israel and Al Jazeera are more specialized news sources since you can evaluate competing viewpoints on Israel vs. Palestinians and/or Arabs. After this was first written, the Washington Post changed its editorial policy to move right, barring some left-wing content and promoting a more libertarian orientation. So far as I know, this did not affect any news sections of the Post. I will reevaluate my paid subscription when the time comes to renew it.

you have such a diversity, you can cross-check stories against each other from those diverse sources, when necessary, which allows you to form a judgment about usual biases and distortions of each news organization.

There is a final set of stories which needs special treatment. It is stories which are part of a religion. Generally, an adherent of one religion believes the stories of that religion to be like news stories about that actual reality while the stories of other religions are complete fiction. The problem is that there is no universal view of what is true about religious stories. Without such a universal view, it is difficult to include religious content as part of actual reality. Yes, religion exists. That is part of reality. You can conduct a scientific investigation of the existence of religion, documenting religion in the way you would any other social phenomenon. But the stories which form the basis of the religion do not have that same agreed quality of being arguably true by most people who consider the matter. Generally, science cannot investigate religious concepts such as Heaven and Hell. They do not exist within the universe, which can be investigated using scientific methods.

Unfortunately, many reporters, who are perhaps adherents of the religion being discussed, are too ready to report a religious story as if it is as factual as any other news story. Reports of bleeding statues, demonic possession, and a host of other topics believed to be true by adherents of some religion are reported as factual happenings, even though scientific investigation denies the reality of all such claims. Later in this book I will discuss the matter of religion in more depth, after we cover some other foundational topics.

But let me reiterate what was said at the beginning of this chapter. Reality exists without the need for any human being whatsoever. If you wish to understand what reality is, try to imagine what would be here if no human being had ever existed. Of course, humans do exist as part of reality. But again, reality does not conform to what human beings believe about it. Reality "just is." Humans might not correctly perceive what reality is. But we should realize that it is a problem with our situation as human beings. It is not a problem with actual reality.

Also, it is an unfortunate attribute of reality that humans frequently try to gain advantage over other humans by forging documents and other media. Such forgeries can be large or small, and they can be easy or difficult to detect.

Modern day experts generally do not have access to original paper documents from thousands of years ago. Instead, what exists today is copies made over many hundreds of years, frequently by medieval monks working in monasteries. These monks sometimes deliberately avoided making an exact copy but instead made alterations favorable to their point of view. One of the most discussed incidences of this type is in the writings of the historian Flavius Josephus.[90] There appear to be at least some alterations made by later copyists in his book *Antiquities of the Jews.*[91] A short passage, called the *Testimonium Flavianum* is the most significant.[92] It purports to provide "contemporary" evidence for the crucifixion of the Christian deity, Jesus Christ. Most modern scholars believe that the passage has some alterations to the original text, but that there was at least some mention of Jesus at that point.[93] But the acknowledged presence of some quantity of forgery in the passage muddies the water about what the reality was of the knowledge of Josephus about Jesus.[94]

---

[90] See https://en.wikipedia.org/wiki/Josephus for his biography.

[91] See https://en.wikipedia.org/wiki/Antiquities_of_the_Jews for a description of the book. The book was written about 93 or 94 CE (perhaps some chapters each year), but no copies have been discovered of the original text. Instead, the earliest surviving portion of a substantial part of the text dates from the 11th century. Smaller excerpts date to the 6th century. The key passage which is debated is quoted by a Christian in the 4th century. The origin of the forgery could be with that 4th century Christian writer, with later copyists using that quote as source material.

[92] See https://en.wikipedia.org/wiki/Josephus_on_Jesus#The_Testimonium_Flavianum for a lengthy discussion.

[93] The main justification for this view is the reference two chapters later to the stoning of "James, the brother of Jesus." If Jesus is not previously mentioned in some substantial way, this identification of James makes no sense.

[94] My opinion is this. The Jewish leader Josephus, who was later adopted into the family of the Roman Emperor, Vespasian, was aware of a Jewish cult (there were many such cults, including the authors of the Dead Sea Scrolls) headed by the brothers Jesus and James, and that Jesus was the better known of the two brothers. Christianity was treated as a cult until it was adopted as the state religion by the Emperor Constantine in the early 4th century. The best argument for the existence of a mention of Jesus in the earlier passage is the later mention of the stoning to death of "James, the brother of Jesus." This mention only makes sense if there were an earlier mention of Jesus. But Josephus was a devout Jew, and was adopted

54

In any case, we can see that some of the stories we receive about reality arrive with some taint of ambiguity about their truth or falsity. How can we tell what is the truth of the matter? That topic is the subject of our next chapter.

---

into the emperor's family, so it would never have crossed his mind to write anything like the *Testimonium*. And that is all you need to know for proof the *Testimonium* was forged.

(THIS PAGE IS INTENTIONALLY BLANK)

CHAPTER 5
HOW DO WE KNOW? SCIENCE

If we think about how humans know things, it largely boils down to two basic methods. First, we know things because other humans tell us, through verbal communication, reading, or other forms of communication. Second, we know things because we investigate them for ourselves. A simple example might be that I step outside to investigate what the current weather is, where I am now. This latter method is a simplified version of a scientific method, consisting of the observation phase of science. If I add some measurement instruments, like a thermometer and a device to measure air pressure, it begins to be an actual scientific investigation. Recording the measurements taken at various times increases the parallels with actual science.

Before you have any ability to make rational decisions of your own, your parents (or some other caregivers) begin to fill your brain with things they think are important for you to know. Usually, that will include the religious beliefs possessed by those people. You adopt your initial religion because it is essentially forced upon you. By the time you are old enough to think rationally about religion, you will not have the mental tools (logic, reasoning, philosophy, etc.) necessary to make an honest decision about your own religious beliefs. Many of those tools are deliberately omitted from modern education.

As a child, you are likely placed into a classroom with other children, most of whom were given similar religious beliefs by their parents. You become part of a "herd" (in some sense) and "herd mentality" keeps you away from heresy. I was raised as a Presbyterian, largely because that was the church near my home which my mother picked to attend. While my peer group included kids from other branches of Christianity, including a few Roman Catholics, I was never seriously exposed to any non-Christian worldview.

What I was exposed to was science fiction. I read Asimov, Clark, Heinlein, and many other classic authors of the genre. In some sense, that opened my mind to alternative worldviews. But the biggest change in my worldview happened almost by accident. I picked up a paperback copy of the science fiction book *Cities in Flight*.[95] It was written by James Blish.[96] After reading through all four novels, I came to the Afterword, which mentions "Oswald Spengler.[97] This was my introduction to Spengler's book *The Decline of the West*.[98] It has been acknowledged by James Blish as one of the sources of *Cities in Flight*." In the early 1980s, I purchased a library card at the University of California, Irvine, and I went there and found a copy on their shelves. As the author of the Afterword said, "Spengler is a difficult thinker – or at least a difficult writer…" I knew I would need time to understand it, so I copied down the identifying information, went to a local bookstore, and ordered a copy of the two-volume set for myself.

When we are young, we are told what to read, and we form our worldview from everything we learn as children. But once we are adults, if we live in a free country, we can expand our worldview with writings from other sources. This is what I did for myself from the mid-1970s through the mid-1990s. I came out of this investigation no longer a Christian.

Ultimately, I adopted the worldview of Thomas Henry Huxley who coined the word "agnostic" to describe his position vis-à-vis religion. This is discussed at length later in the chapter on Religion. In the Introduction to this part, I included the following quote from Huxley:

> *"It is wrong for a man to say that he is certain of the objective truth of any proposition unless he can produce evidence which logically justifies that certainty.*[99]

---

[95] See https://en.wikipedia.org/wiki/Cities_in_Flight for more. I still have a copy of the 1970 edition pictured in that Wikipedia article. The price tag reads "$1.25." I have a fourth printing.

[96] See https://en.wikipedia.org/wiki/James_Blish for more.

[97] See https://en.wikipedia.org/wiki/Oswald_Spengler for Spengler's biography.

[98] See https://en.wikipedia.org/wiki/The_Decline_of_the_West for more. Spengler completed it in 1922, but the English translation wasn't completed until 1928.

[99] Huxley, Thomas, *Agnosticism and Christianity* (1889), essay originally published in the magazine *Nineteenth Century* in May of 1889.

Evidence plus logical justification is the foundation of scientific methods. And it is also the foundation for any claim of truth. This provides the answer to the second question: "How do we know?"

Knowledge which we pass down from one human to another has no inherent truth value. Some Christians claim (without justification) that the Bible "is the literal word of God" (as if God handed down an English version of the King James Bible to Moses, a thought which is absurd on its face). Even some percentage of published scientific papers turn out to be unjustifiable claims (frequently due to methodological mistakes, and occasionally due to outright fraud).[100]

Science produces truth because it is both adversarial and cooperative. The way you get truth out of scientific investigation is to have multiple scientists organized into teams who check each other's work. Even then, science does not always produce the truth, the whole truth, and nothing but the truth. The more competing teams you have producing the same (or similar) results, the more reliance you can place on the findings as being close to the truth.

Good science takes time. It has taken over a century to verify some of the claims Albert Einstein made as part of the two versions of his Theory of Relativity.[101] It also takes huge resources, including billion-dollar telescopes.[102] Also, massive and expensive experimental machines like the Large Hadron Collider.[103] All of these need a commitment, usually by governments, to supply resources for basic research which may or may not produce something of immediate value.

By and large, science does not produce complete and lasting ideas which can in any way be labeled as "ultimate truth." Most results from scientific methods must be categorized as merely tentative, pending any additional information which might come to light if the parameters of the research are changed in some way.

---

[100] One example of this is the scientific paper which claimed vaccines caused autism. After some further investigations did not support the claim, the paper was withdrawn.

[101] See https://en.wikipedia.org/wiki/Theory_of_relativity for an overview.

[102] See the lists of telescopes here: https://en.wikipedia.org/wiki/Telescope which includes sections describing the various types of telescopes used in historical and modern times.

[103] See https://en.wikipedia.org/wiki/Large_Hadron_Collider for a description.

Another reason science cannot produce such results arises from the Problem of Induction.[104] Philosopher David Hume first formulated the problem, essentially proving that we have no reason to expect future experimental results to conform to any theory developed from a set of prior experimental results. Nonetheless, all scientists, and all people, must act as if such predictions are useful, while also recognizing that there is a probability limit to the expectation of conformance to the previously derived theory. We rely upon science because it produces very useful predictions. But we must always remember the influences of probability.

Despite the objections of Hume, the practical results of science throughout all human history force us to declare that science remains as the only set of methods for humans to discover some semblance of the truth. In modern times, we label these as the Scientific Method.[105] Western Civilization, which draws heavily from ancient Greek sources, can trace back to at least Thales of Miletus (c. 626/623 BCE – c. 548/545 BCE).[106] Later writers said he "raises the study of nature from the realm of the mythical to the level of empirical study."[107] Over the next (approximately) 2,500 years, various philosophers, scientists, mathematicians, and others added, changed, and deleted various parts of what eventually John Dewey called "scientific method."[108] While that name is new, the methods were originated as much as many thousands of years ago.

What Dewey described was a general synthesis of roughly 2,500 years of thought on how truth is ascertained by investigations. However, different circumstances can require different procedures, particularly when experimentation isn't possible (i.e., it isn't possible to

---

[104] See https://en.wikipedia.org/wiki/Problem_of_induction for more.

[105] See https://en.wikipedia.org/wiki/Scientific_method for a detailed discussion of this topic.

[106] See https://en.wikipedia.org/wiki/Thales_of_Miletus for more.

[107] Quoted from https://en.wikipedia.org/wiki/Timeline_of_the_history_of_the_scientific_method which see.

[108] Dewey, John (1910), *How We Think*. See https://en.wikipedia.org/wiki/How_We_Think for more.

experiment with exploding a star).[109] Analyzing singular events from long ago is among the most difficult sorts of investigation to conduct. Nonetheless, tools for such analysis do exist, such as Bayesian inference.[110] Somewhat controversially, such methods can even be applied to allegations about singular religious occurrences from thousands of years ago.[111]

The key point here is that scientific methods are adaptable to different circumstances, so long as the principles of careful investigation are adhered to. Science even allows a random chance to play a role, being ready to characterize events in terms of their probability. Science remains as a search for truth, and truth isn't always constrained within preconceived notions.

There are legitimate objections to empirical analysis. Just because Y events always follow X events, there is no universal guarantee that a Y event will always follow an X event without fail. There can be many reasons for failure of this type, including deliberate interference by the observer. Don't bet against a scientist who knows how to manipulate the experiment!

One way of viewing science is that scientific truth is obtained through a rigorous logical and rational analysis of all available and relevant facts. This would include masses of background knowledge obtained by predecessors, even thousands of years into the past. Unless a relevant fact has been disproved later, it must be considered as still relevant, no matter how long ago the fact was documented.

Albert Einstein didn't disprove Newton's Laws of Motion, but he did define circumstances where those laws no longer work as advertised. Newton's Laws still work just fine so long as the observer and the observed do not have a large relative velocity between them. If such a velocity exists, then Newton's laws must be modified in the way

---

[109] We only have one star in our immediate proximity, the Sun, and even if it were possible for humans to cause it to explode, the result would be death for everything on Earth. This is not an experiment which should ever be conducted until and unless humanity has relocated into a different solar system.

[110] See https://en.wikipedia.org/wiki/Bayesian_inference for more.

[111] See Carrier, Richard (2012), *Proving History: Bayes's Theorem and the Quest for the Historical Jesus*.

described by Einstein's equations. Modern science has largely proven Einstein's assertions.

The most common alternative to science is religious belief. Most people alive today have some portion of their thinking contained in an area of their brains described as "religion" while admitting that science produces truth in certain other contexts. This dichotomy is unjustifiable, and that is a central theme of this chapter. The dualism dichotomy should be discarded as an idea unsupported by any facts or logical reasoning. So too the dichotomy of religion and science should be discarded, Gould's Non-Overlapping Magisteria (NOMA) and all. A unified philosophy becomes the framework for science and the replacement for religion, thus eliminating that dual existence.

The warfare of science with theology continues unabated within Western Civilization, as discussed in previous chapters. The so-called "radical religious right" is still attempting to replace the teaching of evolutionary biology with some form of religious creationism in our schools. If they succeed, it will be disastrous for human survival, as understanding evolutionary principles is foundational knowledge to be able to develop things like vaccines against viral infections. Evolution is the reason we need different vaccines each year for things like flu and COVID.

I am not one of the atheists who have asserted that religion has no value for humanity. Religion does have value. But the value is not related at all to the ascertainment of truth. Instead, the value provided by religion comes from the bonds forged among groups of religious adherents and the help which they naturally provide to each of their fellow adherents because of such bonds. I will deal with religion more comprehensively in a later chapter.

Regardless of the truth claims of religion, science is the only proven way to evaluate the truth of any matter. If religion and science produce conflicting truth claims, such as the debate over evolution vs. creationism, science wins every time if the standard for judgement is whether the claim is true and if the judges are truly impartial.

We can return to Ayn Rand's thought experiment. You wake up in an unfamiliar place. What is the first thing that you do? Pray for someone to save you? Or investigate your circumstances? The former is a religious response, and if you choose that option, you are less likely to survive, in part because nobody is listening to your prayers and thus you will receive nothing by praying. Prayer is good for you only in the sense that it conditions your mind towards action. You might as well jump right to act now if you are in any kind of danger. If you choose to investigate, you are following the principles of scientific methodology, and that increases the likelihood of your survival. You might discover danger and a way to mitigate it. The choice is yours.

(THIS PAGE IS INTENTIONALLY BLANK)

CHAPTER 6
WHAT DO WE DO NEXT? SURVIVE!

I discussed previously Ayn Rand's essay *Philosophy, Who Needs It*.[112] It simplified the three most important ideas of philosophy into three questions: 1) What do I know? 2) How do I know it? And 3) What do I do next? Those three questions correspond to the philosophical topics of metaphysics, epistemology, and ethics. To have a consistent philosophy, your ethical standards should be grounded in your stances about metaphysics and epistemology.

For example, if your religious deity commands you and your fellows to kill all infidels who insult the deity, then that becomes an ethical obligation grounded in the beliefs of your religion.

Ayn Rand also described a version of the "package-deal fallacy."[113] It is where a person is asked to adopt a package of essentially different concepts or ideas which are treated as though they are essentially similar. Any major religion involves a package-deal of beliefs. The Christian Bible contains some parts which appear to be historical, some parts which predict the future, some parts which relate the performance of miracles, and some parts which set forth ethical commandments or rules. All those parts are claimed to be the word of God, and believers are expected to adopt that entire package of metaphysical, epistemological, and ethical stances as a "package-deal" to call yourself a Christian. The difficulty for believers is that the Bible is not internally consistent (being the writings of dozens of authors over many centuries), so it is usually quite easy to find opposing texts on the same topic, particularly when comparing parts of the Old and New Testaments. If you adopt Christianity, you fill your mind with a mass of contradictory ideas.

And I don't mean to pick on Christianity. Other major religions (such as Hinduism, Buddhism, and Islam) are worse in my opinion. Still, from their earliest days as thinking people, most children will

---

[112] See https://en.wikipedia.org/wiki/Philosophy:_Who_Needs_It for a summary.
[113] https://en.wikipedia.org/wiki/Package-deal_fallacy#Alternative_interpretation

have some version of a "package-deal" (religion) inculcated into their thinking which unavoidably becomes their philosophy. This is how the civilized religion of society is promulgated from one generation to the next. And, arguably, it helps civilization survive. But there are usually many unintended consequences. For instance, both Islam and Christianity believe in an afterlife which begins with a judgment by God. This leads to a bias in favor of just killing people and letting God rectify any mistakes in the afterlife.[114] If it turns out there is no afterlife after all, there is no fixing any mistaken killings.

Ayn Rand had a lot of good ideas, but she took a wrong turn with her ethical stance. Or at least her most ardent followers did so. Rand centered her discussion of ethics (What do I do next?) on her concept of selfishness, defined as concern for one's own interests. She pointed out that there is no moral component to that concept. It is natural to be selfish in that way.

The wrong thinking arises when you elevate that sort of selfishness (concern for one's own interests) so high in your moral hierarchy that you renounce concern for others living within your society, and that leads to a disintegration of social relationships in society. Such a stance is not only unhealthy, but it can also lead to moral atrocities. To some degree, utilitarianism can be subject to similar objections, but it at least raises concerns about the effects on others of any given choice. Rand's objectivism admits of no such concerns. In some sense Rand is like Gordon Gekko proclaiming that "greed is good." To be honest, Rand disclaims that my objections are real. But many of her followers do not accept the nuanced stance which she wrote about.

If Rand erred in selecting her moral hierarchy, then what is the proper choice? As an atheist, I've been challenged to show that there is an objective foundation for ethics in the absence of some commanding deity. I assert that the foundation of ethical behavior is survival. Frankly, it's a forced choice. Any living thing which does not value survival will tend to die off more rapidly than those who do, and that

---

[114] This argument is sometimes heard in discussions of more rapidly executing people who have been condemned to die because a mistaken execution is no big deal since God will take care of the mistake later.

will rapidly remove such an entity from the gene pool. As humans are the result of billions of years of selection for survival, we ought to realize that the desire for survival (for ourselves, our loved ones, and for our communities of interest) is an innate quality of being human.

Take, as an example, the situation where your child is in danger and is likely to die if you do not intervene. But if you do intervene, you are likely to die in place of the child. What do you do? Rand says you should be concerned mostly with your own interests. If one of you is going to die, should it be the child or you? You can have another child, but you can't have another you. So, you allow your child to die. Most people in Western Civilization would think that was a moral atrocity. Survival is enhanced if the old are sacrificed for the benefit of the young. Self-interest leads you to do the opposite and sacrifice the young for your benefit. In this case, you've decided based upon an incorrect moral hierarchy.

So, what is the correct moral hierarchy? I would suggest the following:

1) Concern for the survival of all life on Earth.
2) Concern for humanity and the ecology needed to support humanity.
3) Concern for the nation or local group(s) with which I most feel affinity for.
4) Concern for my family (spouse, children, etc.) and/or friends.
5) Concern for my own interests.

We expect people to be willing to sacrifice themselves for the good of their nation. The idea of a draft to join the military is based upon that expectation. And history records many cases of volunteers rushing to join the military when war breaks out. As discussed above, we expect a parent to sacrifice themselves for the good of their children. The essence of the modern ecology movement (battling climate change, among other things) is that all nations must be prepared to sacrifice somewhat for the survival of humanity. The reason for stating the hierarchy in this order is that failure at any higher level in the hierarchy automatically fails all lower levels in the hierarchy. If the ecology needed to support humanity is wiped out, then the survival of nations, groups, families, and individuals will all end automatically. This hierarchy is forced. It is not a choice.

The Golden Rule is grounded in the need for survival expressed by the above hierarchy. It is a more formal way of saying "you should have concern for, and be nice to, the people you live with." The purpose of "niceness" in this context is to promote harmony and "teamwork" amongst the participants in any family, group, nation, or an entire civilization.

Religions were designed for largely illiterate peasants. So, religion would have a set of rules which people were expected to memorize (to some degree or another). No reasons were given for the rules. It was just "the rules are the rules, follow them – or else." Sometimes the "or else" is explicit, such as the Christian assertion that you will go to Hell for your afterlife if you commit "blasphemy against the Holy Spirit" (Mark 3:28-29).[115]

In Chapter 3 I mentioned the Last Universal Common Ancestor (LUCA).[116] This is a scientific concept where all living things share some amount of DNA.[117] And it leads to a conclusion that all living things are "cousins" in some sense of that word. These living things were not individually created by a deity but evolved through well-understood mechanisms of descent with modification in the presence of natural selection, which we call "evolution."[118]

Human DNA proves that all humans alive today have common male and female ancestors which, for cultural reasons involving the bias towards a Judeo-Christian religion, are commonly called "Adam" and

---

[115] Different sects of Christianity have different standards for the forgiveness of sin. In some evangelical sects, all you need to do to be forgiven is to show up for a church service, proclaim your belief in Jesus, and all your sins will instantly be forgiven. Roman Catholics usually require confession of sin and the performance of an assigned penance for all except the one unforgivable sin of "blasphemy against the Holy Spirit."

[116] Again, see https://en.wikipedia.org/wiki/Last_universal_common_ancestor for more.

[117] DeoxyriboNucleic Acid (DNA), see https://en.wikipedia.org/wiki/DNA for more.

[118] See https://en.wikipedia.org/wiki/Evolution for a lengthy article, which refers to LUCA.

"Eve." The reference leads to the false conclusions that these two people were a couple and the only humans alive at the time (which derives from the Bible Book of Genesis). The truth is that these people (Adam and Eve) most likely lived thousands of years apart, in different locations, and neither was the only human alive at the time.[119] It is just that through random processes of natural selection, those two people are the only two people who are the last common male and last common female ancestors of all living people today.[120] Every identifiable population today has a similar pair of the last common male and last common female ancestors of that population. Of course, when we get down towards the present, we tend to have genealogical records showing exactly who those people are (it is very likely you know your parents and probably your grandparents, but further back requires more study).[121]

Conceptually we need to extend those thoughts into the distant past and realize that through accidents of time and place those populations split from other similar populations to become distinct groups of people. And the closer we get to the present, the closer are the "cousin" relationships between individuals of such a group. The DNA record is a high-level schematic of the genealogical record since each genetic mutation represents one-to-many generations of humans. With enough information, we can map the DNA relationships onto the family tree from a paper trail.

---

[119] See https://en.wikipedia.org/wiki/Mitochondrial_Eve#/media/File:MtDNA-MRCA-generations-Evolution.svg for a chart of how one woman out of many eventually becomes the last common female ancestor of all people alive today. It is just that the female lines of descent of the other women alive at the same time all died out and this one woman was the last woman whose DNA exists in all women alive today. A similar chart works for men in that there is one man who is the last man whose DNA survives in all men alive today, but he was not the only man alive at the time he was born.

[120] See https://www.nature.com/articles/nature.2013.13478 for a 2013 paper on this topic. The male "Adam" is described at https://en.wikipedia.org/wiki/Y-chromosomal_Adam and he lived roughly 160,000 to 300,000 years ago. "Eve" is described at https://en.wikipedia.org/wiki/Mitochondrial_Eve and she lived in a similar timeframe of roughly 140,000 to 200,000 years ago. This is based upon analysis of surviving genomes and there is no need for "Adam" and "Eve" to have known each other or to have even been alive at the same time or to have been in the same location, other than that generally they should have lived among the earliest human populations in Africa.

[121] I am deeply involved with genealogy, studying both paper trail and DNA evidence to ascertain what might be said about my ancestors.

Accordingly, what are the implications for ethics? First, when we deal with other people, we are dealing with our (likely very distant) cousins. We should always give other people the benefits we would naturally give to at least a distant cousin. Second, I can have some sympathy for people who choose not to eat animals since those animals are closer cousins to us than are the plants.[122]

Third, and most importantly, we need to get away from these ethical systems based upon ancient superstitions and look at adopting an ethical system which is scientifically justifiable.

And that returns me to my earlier discussion in this chapter of my suggested moral hierarchy and the Golden Rule. The moral hierarchy is justified by the genetic relationships I have just described, plus our own survival needs, which in turn requires the survival of an entire ecosystem of creatures who are also our *"cousins"* in the broadest possible sense. The Golden Rule is justified by sociological studies about how societies work best and the scientifically known historical knowledge that some versions of the Golden Rule are known to have existed in nearly all successful human civilizations with a recorded history. Most people get their ethics from their religious tradition. And, as I said in a previous chapter,

"It appears that the underlying purpose is to increase the harmony and smooth functioning of a body of people living as a part of a nation."

Thus, whether we call it a religion or not, we need some sort of frequently recurring universal experience to inculcate ethical values into the population and to call out unethical behavior whenever and wherever it is observed. If it is applied universally, it will lead to a more survivable situation for all humans.

---

[122] But we must eat something. While I would never entertain eating humans (cannibalism) except in the most extreme circumstances, I do not have similar objections for our much more distant bovine cousins who are explicitly raised for the purpose of feeding humans. This is where I differ from my vegan friends who choose to eat only our more-distant cousins, the plants. It is all a matter of degree.

Finally, to circle back to the beginning of this discussion of the value of survival, this thought should be considered:

> *"That life is worth living is the most necessary of assumptions and, were it not assumed, the most impossible of conclusions."*
> – George Santayana, The Life of Reason, 1905.
> From the series Great Ideas of Western Man.

As discussed earlier, it is impossible to fully justify any system of philosophy. Some assumptions must be made. For ethics, the base lies with the biological urge to survive. But intellectually, we could do worse than to adopt this saying of Santayana. Each of us has a life worth living, if only our fellow human beings would treat us according to the Golden Rule.

(THIS PAGE IS INTENTIONALLY BLANK)

CHAPTER 7
RELIGION

I have postponed the discussion of religion because when you adopt a religion, you also adopt a complete philosophy. Each religion comes with sets of metaphysical, epistemological and ethical commandments. For instance, look at the Christian Bible, which begins with the Jewish Torah. The metaphysical worldview varies a lot between the Book of Genesis and the Book of Revelation. There are many places in that Bible which discuss truth. My favorite is John 8:32:

> *"Then you will know the truth, and the truth will set you free."*

I would precede that verse with a summation of the earlier chapter on knowing the truth, creating the following complete thought (replacing John 8:31 from the original):

> *"If you follow the ways of knowledge, which is scientific method, then you will know the truth and the truth will set you free."*

Once you decide to be an atheist, you no longer need to waste time in church listening to preachers ask for money. And you no longer need to give them money. But what of the attack that if you do not believe in the precepts of Christianity, then you're an atheist and infidel? Thomas Henry Huxley dealt with that same charge in an 1889 essay.[123] It pointed out that if his accuser had accompanied him to Cairo, he too would have been an atheist and infidel in the eyes of the Muslim believers he encountered there.

This illustrates the relative nature of such claims that a person is an unbeliever. If a Christian does not believe in the Hindu religion and gods, and the devout Hindu does not believe in the Christian 3-part god

---

[123] See https://aleph0.clarku.edu/huxley/CE5/Agn.html for the complete text of Huxley's essay, *Agnosticism* (1889).

(Father, Son, and Holy Ghost), they are each an unbeliever in each other's religion. Stephen F. Roberts is attributed with a quote that makes a similar point to the one advanced by Huxley back in 1889:

> *"I contend we are both atheists, I just believe in one fewer god than you do. When you understand why you dismiss all the other possible gods, you will understand why I dismiss yours."*[124]

Huxley's agnosticism, which is principally the application of scientific method to all forms of belief, was defined by Huxley this way:

> *"... that it is wrong for a man to say that he is certain of the objective truth of any proposition unless he can produce evidence which logically justifies that certainty."*[125]

Huxley objected to the idea that agnosticism was any kind of a creed, claiming it to be a method (and it is merely the application of scientific method to thoughts outside of science).

But religion is not without value to motivate people to act for the benefit of the group instead of for their benefit, which is in alignment with the ethical stance I describe earlier in chapter 6. The problem with religion is that the motivation is usually to enhance the power or status of the leader rather than to do actual good. We want soldiers to throw themselves into battle and defeat the opposing forces. Would they do that without the motive of an eternal reward, should they happen to give their lives in this war effort? Would Charles Martel have defeated the much larger Muslim army in 732 if his army had contained only atheists? It is a legitimate question, but one many atheists would challenge since many atheists serve in the military. The old slur that *"there are no atheists in foxholes"* is simply not true. Another question is whether

---

[124] See: https://www.goodreads.com/quotes/17095-i-contend-that-we-are-both-atheists-i-just-believe which contains the quote but does not reference the source. I believe it was from an online debate in the early days of the Internet. But I could be wrong.

[125] See https://aleph0.clarku.edu/huxley/CE5/Agn-X.html for the complete text of Huxley's essay *Agnosticism and Christianity* (1889).

the religiously driven Crusades did any actual good for humanity? I would assert that they did not. But it would lead to a long argument with believers.

On the one hand, religion seems to be a necessary piece of a civilized population. On the other hand, there have been over a dozen civilizations in the history of mankind, each with its own religion, so the specific content of the religion doesn't seem to matter much. What does seem to matter is the cohesiveness and motivation towards common action.

The more a person understands about science, the more difficult it is to choose to be a strong adherent of literal Christianity. One inseparable part of Christianity is belief in demonic possession. The Roman Catholic Church to this day has a professional exorcist on the staff of each diocese to be available to cast out demons from any believer who becomes possessed. There are many verses in the Bible which refer to demonic possession and exorcism. Matthew 8:28-34 tells the story of two demon-possessed men where Jesus cast the demons out into a herd of pigs. Then the pigs promptly ran into the sea and drowned themselves. Luke 8:26-37 tells the same or a similar story.[126] But in both cases the demons are alleged to be spirit entities which can take over a human (or porcine) body (which is what "demonic possession" means).

Do demons like that exist? Only in fiction (i.e., Ghostbusters). A significant cottage industry exists to exploit believers in demons and other spirits, including ghosts. But whenever actual impartial scientists get involved, the demons or spirits never seem to perform as advertised. This is not a new phenomenon. In 1889/90 Thomas Henry Huxley got into a dispute with the great statesman William Gladstone, a true believer in the Bible.[127] They debated these very stories of the swine from

---

[126] There is a significant theological debate over whether Matthew and Luke are discussing the same incident or two distinct incidents that sound very much like each other. The more literal reading you demand of the Bible, the more you will tend to believe that two distinct incidents are described in the two books of the Bible.

[127] Gladstone's mother was an intensely religious follower of the evangelical Scottish Episcopal Church.

Matthew and Luke. Huxley's statement which greatly upset Gladstone was this:

"Everything that I know of law and justice convinces me that the wanton destruction of other people's property is a misdemeanor of evil example" ("Nineteenth Century," February 1889, p. 172).

Here Huxley takes issue with Jesus either giving permission to or ordering the demons to destroy the swine.[128] If you accept that characterization, it may explain why, at the end of each story, Jesus is requested to leave the vicinity. Of course, the authors of these stories could not have Jesus arrested, tried, convicted, and executed for this. Jesus would need to wait to die. But the local people should not tolerate someone who destroys valuable property.

And neither Huxley nor I believe in the existence of a spirit world, and particularly not in a demon-haunted world.[129] In his 1889 essay Agnosticism and Christianity Huxley opined:

"... that, in my judgment, the demonology of primitive Christianity is devoid of foundation; and that no man, who is guided by the rules of investigation which are found to lead to the discovery of truth in other matters, not merely of science, but in the everyday affairs of life, will arrive at any other conclusion."

The millennia of scientific inquiry leading to the modern understanding of scientific method is what leads to the inescapable conclusion that demons do not exist, and because of that, there is no chance of any human being "possessed" by a demon or by the Holy Spirit.[130]

Huxley goes on to explain some of the paradoxical nature of the synoptic Gospels in that some material appears in all three, some

---

[128] The stories in Matthew and Luke differ in this regard.

[129] "Demon-Haunted World" is a 1995 book by Carl Sagan and his wife, Ann Druyan. The book offers a popular explanation of scientific method, and I highly recommend that you should read it.

[130] Claimed instances of such possession have been shown to involve "acting out" by the participants.

material appears in each combination of two out of the three, and some material appears in only one out of the three. Huxley concludes his discussion of the story of the swine with these two paragraphs:

> *It further follows that those who accept devils, posses-sion, and exorcism as essential elements of their concep-tion of the spiritual world may consistently consider the testimony of the Gospels to be unimpeachable in respect of the information, they give us respecting other matters which appertain to that world.*

> *Those who reject the gospel demonology, on the other hand, would seem to be as completely barred, as I feel myself to be, from professing to take the accuracy of that information for granted. If the threefold tradition is wrong about one fundamental topic, it may be wrong about another, while the authority of the single tradi-tions, often mutually contradictory as they are, becomes a vanishing quantity.*

This presents us with the ultimate problem concerning religion. All religion is predicated upon *"revealed truth"* which, when written down, can be compared with the findings of scientific inquiry. Science asserts that no satisfactory evidence of demons or demonic possessions exists. The Bible presents itself as exactly the evidence demanded by science. Unfortunately, for science to find evidence to be acceptable (or satis-factory) it must be observable by an independent observer. Modern-day holy men claim the ability to cast out demons. How about a demonstra-tion of that ability in a controlled environment subject to scientific ob-servation? It will never happen.

I recently re-read Huxley's 1889 essay and discovered a mention that this issue of no modern-day miracles was being investigated by the Church of England, styled as the question of "When did miracles cease to occur?" The true answer to that question is that miracles have never occurred. They are as fictional as any writing about magical happenings in Harry Potter books.

I am most familiar with Christianity as that was the religion of my youth. But I can assure you that each other religion has beliefs in a spirit world which can be similarly challenged. My clear recommendation is that you should not believe in spirit worlds!

Is it reasonable to believe in a spirit world? Huxley would assert that no scientist should ever believe in any such thing because no evidence supports the idea that such a world exists. Spirits and spirit worlds are not a part of reality, as perceived by science. But the many religions of the world employ every linguistic trick available to argue that the existence of such a world cannot be disproved, and so "people of faith" must believe it to be true as an "act of faith." In other words, it is necessary to the con game of most churches that people believe in the fictions which the church preaches. No belief in fiction, no income stream for the preachers!

Western Civilization began when the secular ruler, Charlemagne, was crowned Emperor of the Romans by the religious authority, Pope Leo III. For many centuries there was no other popular religion within the areas dominated by Western Civilization. But the 16th century saw a shattering of the Christian faith into what is now many thousands of sects of Christianity, some large (such as the Catholic Church itself) and some small (in the US, it generally takes only a few followers to be able to form a recognized "church"). Today, sects which call themselves "Christian" span the entire range of possible beliefs such that there is no single belief or set of beliefs which link together all those many sects of Christianity. No matter what core belief you care to select, there is some sect of Christianity somewhere who refuses to believe that core belief. This comes very close to making the words Christian and Christianity entirely meaningless. These essential meaningless religious words fit perfectly with the essential emptiness of Western Culture, which "died" with the dissolution of the Holy Roman Empire. It makes no sense at all to attempt to perpetuate Christianity into the future. Modern Christianity has transformed itself into the enemy of science and rational thought. As such, we must adopt an anti-Christian stance for our survival.

Still, if we are to form a new civilization to rise out of the ashes of Western Civilization, we will need a religion to unify us in our quest for mutual survival. We could do worse than to adopt the agnosticism of Huxley as our philosophical religion for this new civilization.[131] It should produce some interesting results![132]

---

[131] According to Huxley, Agnosticism is essentially the epistemological side of atheism as a metaphysical stance. The two are completely compatible, as Bertrand Russell wrote many decades ago. There are several atheist churches which have been founded in the USA. My "Agnostic Church" selected herein is not significantly different.

[132] The first question, which will take centuries to answer, is whether a reality-based religion will lead to the same sort of cycles of development which Spengler described. I hope not, and I have a lot of reasons why I believe that to be the case.

(THIS PAGE IS INTENTIONALLY BLANK)

PART II

FORWARD PLANNING

A PROGRAM FOR HUMAN SURVIVAL

(THIS PAGE IS INTENTIONALLY BLANK)

PART II
INTRODUCTION

The fundamental inspiration for what we ought to be doing comes from Rodney King, who uttered some memorable comments during a press conference on May 1, 1992, during which he was attempting to stop the violence and looting taking place in Los Angeles after the officers who beat him were acquitted of all charges:

"I just want to say, you know, can we all get along?"

"Please, we can get along here. We all can get along. I mean, we're all stuck here for a while. Let's try to work it out"[133]

We don't need to turn everyone into an obedient robot to just get along with each other. We just need to develop a tolerance for individual differences. Each of us should commit to learning about different people and cultures because, all too frequently, one man's cultural icon is another man's worst nightmare.

A lot of friction comes from religious differences. Some Christians believe the Islamic Quran is filled with blasphemy and want to burn it.[134] You can be offended and express your opinion of offense. But it is not ok to kill the person offending you. We should motivate people to use only peaceful means for resolving offensive conduct. It is an unfortunate truth that people of the Islamic faith have numerous practices which offend sensibilities of those of us raised within Western Civilization. Forced child marriage, honor killings, and killing people for the slightest offense taken by followers of Mohammed, such as the Quran burning just described.

Christianity is supposed to be a religion of peace. However, many horrible wars, including genocidal exterminations, have been justified by Christian scriptures. It is not only Islam which made forced religious conversions at the point of a sword. Killing people should be a last

---

[133] See https://en.wikipedia.org/wiki/Rodney_King#Los_Angeles_riots_and_aftermath for more.
[134] In the alternative, some just deliberately intend to offend Muslims by performative blasphemy.

resort, only justifiable in the gravest of circumstances. And differences of religious opinions should rarely justify such actions. Only if the religious opinion threatens harm under our universal ethical code should any punishment be passed out, and execution as punishment is rarely justifiable.[135]

On the other hand, a true claim of self-defense always justifies a killing. The key word here is "true." There must be an honest justified belief that the person to be killed is attacking someone with the intent to kill before that is a true claim of self-defense. A lot of the problems go away if people are legally discouraged from carrying weapons. So-called "open carry" of firearms is a concept which is guaranteed to lead to more deaths over time.[136]

But getting along should mean more than just not attacking or killing someone who offends you in some way. It should extend to helping a person in need who is part of our community. A so-called "good person" should never be homeless or hungry. Most of us could allow a homeless person to sleep on our couch and a hungry person to share our meals. Not permanently, for sure, but at least in an emergency. This comes from the ethical value of caring for the community within which we live. Someday, it may be your turn to need help. Each of us is only one bad roll of the dice away from homelessness.[137] Even Joe Btfsplk deserves a place to sleep at night.[138] His troubles are not his fault.

On the other hand, we should not tolerate the sort of sociopaths who are always seeking to take advantage of others. Such people are frauds

---

[135] I would personally entertain the idea that a prisoner, sentenced to live in prison without the possibility of parole, who then manages somehow to kill a prison guard, could be a candidate for execution. Another possibility would be a methodical serial killer with multiple greatly premeditated murders over a significant period of time. Such a person is almost certainly an incurable sociopath who will harm others in prison.

[136] Many towns in the old west had rules about checking guns before you could freely travel around town.

[137] I have personally had minor bouts of homelessness. Once I was working "on the road" and the long-term rental (for which I had paid a week in advance) was burned down in a fire. I slept in my car that night. Then I called my boss, and he paid for a new place to stay. Another time I was about to begin a new job, but I arrived in the city with my family and not enough money to pay for a motel. I bought a tent, and we stayed at a campsite in a public park until I got my first paycheck. Not fun. But in a society of good people, such things should not happen.

[138] See https://en.wikipedia.org/wiki/Joe_Btfsplk for a description of this famous cartoon character.

84

and criminals who make their living through lies, deceit, theft, and other criminal activities. Many times, drug addiction is part of what has led these people down the path of antisocial behavior.[139] How can we tell deserving people who are down on their luck from sociopaths who are taking advantage of our generosity? That is a key question, and I have a beginning proposal.

I intend to form a Good People Group (GPG). It will be something like Go Fund Me, in that people can choose to contribute money. But it will also promote "in kind" donations, such as providing a guest room in a home for someone who desperately needs it. An online database will track giving and receiving and allow "YELP-like" rankings of personal reputations. A record of giving to others makes you worthy to receive when your own time of need arrives.

But GPG is not only useful in dealing with personal or community-wide disasters. Many people need childcare, either during a workday for younger children or just after school for older children. Many seniors can contribute to caring for children, and they would be helped by the associated social interaction. Arranging babysitting for a night out could be done using this same system. When an area has enough GPG members, we could even build facilities along the lines of what is offered by Jewish Community Centers.[140] We can arrange to have libraries of uncensored books and add to the education of our children with lessons derived from our own moral principles.

GPG can provide credit union services and recommend honest businesses run by our members. The whole idea is mutual support of our members, by our members, and for the benefit of our members as well as the community at large.

---

[139] This applies to my first wife. Every time I took her to a drug rehab program, she used her time there to learn how to be a better drug addict. After 3 or 4 cycles in and out of rehab, insurance was refusing to pay any more, and she was obviously in a worse state than when she was first admitted. When her path became clear to me, I had to divorce her, for the sake of both of us. Eventually she found a different path, and the last I heard she was still alive. Many drug addicts do not survive.

[140] One thing to investigate is whether or not we could have non-Jewish members use such facilities in places where they exist, but GPG facilities do not.

In some real sense, GPG can be a "virtual village" for raising our kids to be good people themselves. If we are building a new society to replace The West, we will want that society to be populated with good people. And the best way to get more good people is to raise them from childhood to be good people. If some child turns out to be a sociopath instead of a good person, that child can be shunned by the remaining good people. Let them make their own way in the dog-eat-dog world of Western capitalism.

Every society has a strong religious component, and our new society needs more than just good people to train our kids. The next piece of the movement is to form an actual Agnostic Church organization to provide religious services to the good people. Physical facilities can include Agnostic Church activities as part of the same facilities used for GPG. Adherents of other religions can be good people, but Agnostic Church members are morally required to be good people. Thus, Agnostic Church membership is a step up from merely belonging to GPG.

Legally, GPG should be organized as a "mutual benefit" cooperative (or co-op). This type of organization has a long history, but it is useful for ordinary people to band together in opposition to the oppressive business interests which would otherwise take advantage of individual members of the co-op. Co-ops are best known in farming communities, but they have been used in urban contexts as well.

On the other hand, the Agnostic Church should be organized as an actual church, with all the tax privileges and benefits usually associated with a church of any denomination. Tax exemptions will be particularly useful when we begin to build our community centers. We have complete freedom to develop our training programs for ourselves and our children. They can be both educational and entertaining.

The financial model should be based on that used by the Roman Catholic Church and/or the Latter Day Saints (LDS), but with more diversity of control. Ownership of church funds and properties should be vested in local clergy as trustees for the global church body. The global body can force the removal and/or replacement of local trustees whenever necessary or desirable, and intermediate supervisory bodies can be created when desirable for more "local control" of the lower-level churches. And the hierarchy of local trustees can vote on the leadership for the next higher level. But because ownership is diffused by area, region, nation, etc., no one autocrat can act to seize all the assets of the Agnostic Church. The largest bank accounts should be kept in banks in the safest of nations. Until we achieve our domination, we must always keep in mind the possibility of needing to escape from a bad situation.

The Catholic Church has an all male fraternal organization called the Knights of Columbus.[141] The idea for the Agnostic Church is to have a Huxley Society, including both men and women, to provide more activism around growing the movement. Leaders are grown through participating in creating and implementing activities which demonstrate our commitment to our values. We also want to recruit more good people to join GPG and the Agnostic Church.

The three organizations described above can form the beginning of a new society that draws good people into its orbit and evolves as necessary for future needs. It is a foundation, and not a limit. More things can be developed as needs grow.[142] As we add services for our members, we can work into those services the principles of GPG. For instance, no member should lose insurance coverage because they are out of a job and can't pay the premiums.[143]

Western capitalism is deliberately cruel. Seeking profit without other considerations means taking advantage of people as much as possible with every interaction. When profit is the sole objective, cruelty

---

[141] See https://www.kofc.org/en/who-we-are/our-story/index.html for its main website. That page states its mission as "empowering Catholic men to live their faith at home, in their parish, at work and in their community." Also see https://en.wikipedia.org/wiki/Knights_of_Columbus for a more neutral description of the group.

[142] I have already proposed a credit union. The Knights of Columbus have an insurance arm and financial advisors. Those are natural additions as we grow large enough to support them.

[143] In the United States, you should have COBRA available to pay for healthcare, but the premiums are often so high that an unemployed person can't make those payments. GPG should provide some sort of "payment insurance" coverage to help people in such circumstances, particularly where there are known health issues.

becomes the byproduct.[144] Good people reject that as an immoral principle. Instead, we believe that kindness towards others, as commanded by the Golden Rule, is the proper foundation for commercial interactions. By banding together, many small contributions can be aggregated into massive benefits for those who find themselves in need. Or we can at least avoid the cruel part of making profits in our business activities.

Join us and make it so.

To get things going, I've set up an online presence using my Agnostic Church domain name. Please join here:

https://www.agnostic.org/

---

[144] The similar phrase "the cruelty is the point" has frequently been used to describe President Trump's policies because those policies seem mostly designed to injure people to demotivate them from acting against Trump's wishes. Either way, cruelty is being inflicted to achieve an unrelated objective.

CHAPTER 8
ECONOMICS

History tells us that a civilization begins with a society growing out of the agricultural revolution. Thus, there is some farming system, carried out using either socialistic or feudalistic principles. The basic idea of our new civilization is to entirely skip over the feudalistic beginnings of most civilizations and jump right into an advanced economy with an established merchant class.

That does not mean we will be ignoring the socialistic principles of some advanced nations within Western Civilization. But we will ground our socialistic aspects using our moral standards, thus creating an economic form I will call "moral capitalism."

Moral capitalism contrasts with the so-called "laissez-faire" capitalism of the United States and most other nations in the world of Western Civilization. The principles of "laissez-faire" capitalism exalt profits at any moral cost. A recent study showed that this attitude increases the death rate of healthcare patients, killing actual people by forcing cost reductions.[145]

Moral capitalism is what we should have had in the democratic era of Western Civilization, but which we mostly did not have because we gave too much power to those who control the money. Declaring that "corporations are people" is an immoral stance.[146] Corporations should not have any rights vis-a-vis a living human being beyond the ability to enforce contracts up until a court judgement holds otherwise (for instance, during a bankruptcy proceeding).

Donald Trump hails himself as displaying "The Art of the Deal." But an honest evaluation of his business practices concludes that it is

---

[145] Hannah Harris Green, in The Guardian, 6 Feb 2025, *US health department condemns private equity firms for role in declining healthcare access*.

[146] Corporations are business partnerships where the owners cannot be individually sued absent certain kinds of corrupt conduct, like taking corporate assets for personal use or enrichment. You can't put a corporation into jail, so it does not deserve to be treated as a separate and distinct "person." Only actual biological people are "people."

more "The Art of the Steal." Trump is well known for not paying vendors until or unless they take him to court and invest the money necessary to force him to pay. For most small companies, the cost of a lawsuit is more than the value of the debt to be collected. And a lawsuit against Trump always runs the risk of an expensive countersuit over some imagined injury. Trump is devoid of moral principles.

Whatever we develop as a legal system for our new civilization, it must strongly discourage making frivolous claims or defenses in court. At a minimum, a losing plaintiff should be forced to pay all the costs of defending a frivolous claim, with the judge (or a jury if it gets to trial) granted the power to determine whether a losing claim was frivolous, and to what degree. Similarly, a losing defendant should be forced to pay all the costs of a plaintiff where there is no defense raised which is not frivolous. The law should encourage early settlement of business litigation, with formal settlement offers made by each side. At the eventual end of the case, the result should be compared to the recorded settlement offers and the costs of the litigation paid by all parties should be divided according to who gained the most and the least by forcing the litigation to proceed beyond the amount offered in the settlements offered at the beginning of the court case. If the gain was small, or even negative, and the costs were huge, then the burden of paying those costs for all sides should fall upon the party who gained nothing substantial as compared to the original settlement offer. And given the preference for arbitration in our modern economy, good people can establish our own system of arbitration to resolve disputes using our own moral principles. Big corporations use arbitration to their own advantage. So can we.

Attorneys in litigation ought to be held to standards not of extreme advocacy, but instead to standards of honesty and truth, more like British barristers. It should be up to these advocates to work with both sides towards a settlement, if possible, all the time reminding the parties that they represent that they will pay the costs of pursuing a frivolous claim or defense if it is unlikely to produce a result substantially more favorable than an early settlement offer from other parties.

Another concept to consider is whether wealthy parties like Trump ought to be forced to file a litigation bond for any new litigation after they have previously been ordered to pay litigation costs to another party. Anything should be considered if it cuts down frivolous litigation.

But litigation costs are not the main villain in our economy. The worst aspect of the modern economy is the drive by businesses at all levels to produce larger profits without consideration of the costs or injuries inflicted upon customers, vendors and/or employees. In some sense it is a species of fraud to raise prices to consumers when no extra value is provided. Similarly, it is a species of fraud to require more productivity from workers when no additional compensation is given. Productivity gains ought to be rewarded by paying out some agreeable percentage of increased profits to the workers who increased their productivity.

Workers are stakeholders in the business just as much as owners or shareholders or managers might be. All stakeholders should be fairly compensated out of profits for the contribution(s) which are made towards the success of the business. Where unions exist, they should be modeled more on the German system as opposed to the "seek maximum advantage for our side" system in the United States. This means much more cooperation towards creating a successful strategy for any business between workers and managers to benefit all stakeholders.

The taxes necessary to support social services ought to be automatically adjusted to meet the needs of those receiving said services. A rate fixed decades ago is probably not adequate to meet the needs of current beneficiaries, particularly when demographic trends are increasing the population of beneficiaries. It isn't the case that these demographic trends were hidden. We've known that the "baby boom" was working its way towards the age of Social Security since at least the 1950s. But politicians hate to be known for raising taxes, particularly when they raise taxes on those who can easily afford to pay. Those people usually are a large part of the influence team who lobbies legislatures for lower taxes for people like themselves. If an automatic formula is used, with full transparency as to the cash inflows and outflows, it becomes much harder to interfere with the tax rates paid by those who lobby against them.

All forms of cryptocurrency should be illegal. Cryptocurrency is mostly used for criminal activity. Ransomware would be a lot more difficult of an occupation if Bitcoin was illegal to use. Also, there should eventually be only one form of money in use worldwide. All governments would need to cooperate in maintaining full faith and credit for the global currency, which should be managed in a way like how the Euro is managed now. With global currency, the business of money changing would disappear. That eliminates a drag on economic activity.

The economy should be run using principles derived from our moral values, including versions of the Golden Rule. A nursing home should treat each patient like a person would treat their own parent. Not like the patient is a profit center which should produce a maximal profit.

Another idea comes from the "leave a penny, take a penny" dish which I used to see near cash registers when I was young. In the modern economy, the penny is nearly obsolete, and I expect it to be eliminated as part of the US monetary system soon. But the concept can be resurrected by the "round-up" plea at checkout. At McDonald's you are asked to "round-up" to support the Ronald McDonald House charity. The video screens for checkout could easily be programmed with a short list of charities, including the "leave a penny" charity, which would allow people to contribute to a pot of money, which could be used to complete a purchase under certain circumstances.[147]

---

[147] One example might be that a person paying with a SNAP card comes up $1.55 short for goods that qualify for SNAP. The "round-up" fund would be tapped to pay that $1.55. Setting the qualifications for and limits for such payments would require further study. And these could be automatically adjusted according to the amount of money currently available in the fund.

It should be obvious by now that the main ethos of a retail store should be to treat customers like they are members of your own family. This attitude dominated not too many decades ago. I'm certain that kind of approach was there for my great-grandfather who ran a corner general store on the ground floor of the house his family lived in. As our economy has moved from ownership by individual proprietors to ownership by corporate behemoths like Walmart, any consideration of personal warmth towards the people paying their money has completely vanished.

Centuries ago, a craftsman was judged by the quality of his product (among other things). Today, product engineers are instructed to make products cheaply, and to ensure that they do not last too long. Customers in the West are encouraged to replace products as quickly as possible. You can see this change in something as simple as a light bulb. I visited Edison's home in Fort Myers, FL, and some of his original bulbs were still burning decades after Edison's death. Those bulbs didn't receive the "wear out on schedule" treatment because they were among Edison's first bulbs. Modern bulbs come with a stated lifetime of some number of hours of illumination. The customer should have a choice between "cheap" and "long-lasting." Maybe not from the same manufacturer, but let the marketplace decide what best suits the customer's needs.

One thing which should go away is the "incredible shrinking product." A "pound" of butter that weighs only 15 or 14 ounces. A large bag of potato chips that is more than half full of air and weighs half an ounce less than it did a month ago. We need to view these products as a species of fraud. A "pound" should be exactly 16 ounces, just like we learn in math class. If the weight or quantity of a product in a package changes, that change must be prominently advertised on the package for at least a year. To just let the consumer find out what happened by reading the fine print and comparing an old and a new package, that is a species of fraud.

The modern economy is centered around maximizing profits for heartless corporations with no morality, just the greedy seeking of profits, inflicting fraud upon its customers and workers alike. Maximizing profits means charging the highest possible prices while paying the lowest possible wages, plus the lowest possible prices to any vendors. To Ayn Rand, this greed was the epitome of virtue. To me, this is the height of immorality. A business should not exist solely to inflict fraudulent damages upon all who deal with it.

A recent article in the New York Times had this quote about why fire engines were too expensive and took too long to purchase:

> *"At the end of the day, absent competition, monopoly capitalism is a shakedown."*[148]

Public corporations are strongly motivated by Wall Street to seek the maximum amount of profit regardless of moral costs. It is not a bit surprising that their business practices are comparable to a Mafia shakedown. Frito Lay is the only large supplier of snack foods because when Anheuser-Busch tried to compete with it, using part of its vast beer fortune to create Eagle Snacks, Frito Lay responded with every trick in the book to run Busch out of the snack food business. Coke and Pepsi have a decades-long truce as the dual suppliers of soda pop. Every large business does everything possible to create a monopoly or duopoly (or even a triopoly) with unspoken tacit agreements to milk the market for all possible profits. Who gets hurt the most? Consumers, of course.

Sharp business practices gradually migrate into outright business fraud. That is part of how the current President of the United States made his fortune. He seems to have scammed his family members.[149]

---

[148] Edward Kelly, general president of the International Association of Fire Fighters, quoted in The New York Times, *As Wall Street Chases Profits, Fire Departments Have Paid the Price*, by Mike Baker, Maureen Farrell and Serge F. Kovaleski, 17 Feb 2025, accessed on the web (paywall) at: https://www.ny-times.com/2025/02/17/us/fire-engines-shortage-private-equity.html

[149] It is well documented that Donald kept the children of his deceased brother Fred, Jr. from inheriting an equal portion of his father's estate. Donald also seems to have cut his surviving siblings in for a far

He also famously stiffed his vendors. And yet he was so incompetent of a businessman that he drove his Atlantic City casinos into bankruptcy. The root cause of this was a despicable combination of huge greed and larger ego. I should note that the Christian religion normally preaches in favor of humility and generosity.[150] But the modern Christian church is more centered on greed. The preacher needs a larger salary, and he also wants to add to the building(s) which he controls through the church which he runs. So-called megachurches draw techniques from advertising and marketing to attract crowds to fill the pews. And once the pews are full, it is time to milk the people for money. Is that what Jesus would have done? Of course not, but Jesus isn't returning to call these false prophets to task.

In the early years of The West, the feudal system meant that power generated money. In the recent later years, money generates power.[151] But it is not many years into the future when the powerful figure out that they can just take all the money they want. This is what Spengler meant when he predicted the "victory of force-politics over money." Putin already operates that way. He already has a record of eliminating wealthy people who offend him through exile, prison, or death. The remainder of the world is headed towards that same end. The only question is what will the people do about it?

So long as we still have some degree of freedom, we can find ways to create our economy, divorcing our economic activities from the greed of those we live with. We do not need to be ostentatious about it. We can build a moral economy "under the radar" until we have enough members to head off in a different direction. Hopefully, the good people who read this book will recognize that we ought to live as much of our lives as possible in a state of morality by our own definition. If we cannot, we should consider ourselves to be "in prison" within Western

---

smaller part of his father's estate than an equal division would have provided. Basically, Donald took everything he could.

[150] These virtues are not frequently kept by the purported practitioners of Christianity. The so-called "prosperity Gospel" is based on approximately the reverse of those virtues.

[151] Just look at what Elon Musk is doing after he purchased Trump's election.

Civilization, and it should be our goal to destroy those prison walls as soon as we can safely do so.

The immoral capitalism within which we live strives to break down families into competing individuals, each of whom is expected to pay their way to the lords of business who run their lives. This is the antithesis of a group mutually caring for each other, which should be the goal of our moral capitalism. Some good ideas along these lines were advanced by former First Lady (and Secretary of State) Hillary Rodham Clinton in her book *It Takes a Village*.[152] Clinton was focused on the needs of children. But we should expand upon her ideas to create a system of cradle to grave care within our own self-chosen "village" (which might be virtual as well as physical).

As the greed of immoral capitalism, acting through its agents of Trump and Musk, slashes and burns its way through government, most "social safety net" programs are destined for the trash heap. And most of them were inadequate to the need in the first place. Take "Meals on Wheels" as an example. The federal government funds about one third of its operations through the Older Americans Act Nutrition Program.[153] If Trump and Musk cut that funding, how many senior citizens will lose their services? We are entering an era where immoral capitalists (led by Musk) are demanding that our government end all government-paid charity. The people must respond by increasing their support for charitable causes.

But these same older Americans can be a tremendous resource for the community. One of the largest needs for parents is affordable daycare for children. Why not recruit able older Americans to help with daycare in return for providing them meals?[154] Maybe the "wheels" part

---

[152] See https://en.wikipedia.org/wiki/It_Takes_a_Village for more.
[153] See https://www.mealsonwheelsamerica.org/learn-more/national/press-room/news/2017/03/16/statement-clarifying-federal-funding-to-meals-on-wheels for more.
[154] One downside to this idea is that these meals would amount to a taxable "in kind" compensation. But for eligible seniors, that should not create a tax problem as they would generally be too poor for such income to be taxes. Still, they may need a program of help submitting income tad forms.

can turn into transportation for those who cannot drive. There is a solution here just waiting to be born.

Almost every area of the modern economy rips off consumers in some fashion. And yet, we just seem to take it. Still, it makes us mad, which leads to an overall reservoir of deep-seated anger that drives us all further apart from one another. The solution is to divorce ourselves as much as possible from the monopoly players.

The food industry is one of the worst as the monopolists generally control the middlemen. They pay low prices to the farmers and set high prices for the consumers. There are too many farmers to effectively negotiate, and the middlemen end up with most of the profits.

As we begin to envision establishing our own private "economy" we will need infrastructure in the way of facilities where to perform all these activities. If you look around in your community, you should see such facilities widely available. They are called "churches" (or other similar names, like synagogues or mosques). Most churches have some sort of community space within their buildings. A set of school classrooms (for Sunday School, for instance) can become a preschool or an alternative school during the day. Jewish Community Centers provide a wide variety of activities separate and apart from the religious properties. You ought to be able to obtain healthy exercise close to your home without needing to patronize a corporate owner attempting to extract the maximum amount of money possible. Such a facility becomes the perfect location for childcare and senior care working together.

Such a facility could also be used for distributing goods and services acquired through a co-op purchasing scheme. We can bypass at least one layer of the retail system by purchasing wholesale the things that are popular for the local population.

I'm certain that there are hundreds if not thousands of ideas that could be used to cut costs and increase the value received for members of our community. But first, we need to have a community in a local area where enough of us live to significantly help each other. And the remaining chapters in this part will deal with aspects of creating that community.

CHAPTER 9
A PLAN OF ACTION

Let me first summarize some conclusions for all of us to understand and articulate:

1. The guidelines for moral action are rooted in the hierarchy discussed in the previous chapter on ethics. To summarize, we begin with the idea that we each possess a life worth living (with some rare exceptions, including the possibility of assisted suicide in justifiable circumstances). If that is true, our living should be guided by allocating our moral focus as noted within the following hierarchy of moral concerns:

   a. Concern for the survival of life on Earth (all living things at the species level).

   b. Concern for humanity and the ecology needed to support humanity.

   c. Concern for the nation or local group(s) with which I most feel affinity for.

   d. Concern for my family (spouse, children, etc.) and/or friends.

   e. Concern for my own interests, including my own happiness.

2. The economic principles of capitalism have proven themselves to be valuable to humanity through vast scientific and economic benefits. However, we only obtain good value if we constrain capitalism according to moral principles and thus create an economy of *"moral capitalism."*

3. Wealthy people are not inherently bad, but they should not be allowed to use their wealth to do bad things, and they must pay their fair share of taxes to the government.

4. The goal of moral capitalism is the good, defined as fairness, liberty, and justice for all, which is all grounded in the Golden Rule.

5. Both extreme socialism and extreme capitalism are evil. The true goal of moral capitalism ought to be to balance between those extremes to maximize the good and minimize the evil.

6. A balance between socialism and capitalism provides the best situation for the most people. Minimize evil, maximize good, and people will be the happiest they can be.

7. A balanced program of moral capitalism is a populist program which people from both sides of the political spectrum (left and right) ought to support.

8. Like Barry Goldwater, moral capitalism opposes concentrations of power, public or private. Such concentrations impede or prevent fairness, liberty, and justice for all. Monopolies of any kind (economic, cultural, or governmental) can be evil and must be either eliminated or tightly regulated to prevent evil.

9. Science produces truth, and truth trumps religious and political opinions when it is well substantiated. Government paying for science is a socialist program to better humanity.

When properly explained, moral capitalism ought to be desired by every thinking voter. The United States has never been without some form of socialism. In the earliest decades, land was made available to men at little or no cost so they could farm. Today, family farming is no longer the bedrock of economic activity in the United States. So, what benefits people today is vastly different than the benefits people sought centuries ago. It is easy to forget that the idea of germs was unknown before the middle of the 19th century. Just think of the benefits to people from the discovery that germs make people sick. Pure capitalism also makes people sick or even die. Imposing morality upon capitalism tries to prevent much of that evil.

Religion is another source of evil within Western Civilization. The Roman Catholic Church is not the only religious organization which has been plagued by numerous scandals involving sexual abuse. And we all know of some megachurch preachers who seem most concerned with their own wealth and power rather than the well-being of members of their congregations.

There is hardly any area of Western Civilization which isn't sick to some degree or another with some evil according to the moral standards which I list above. We have an immoral version of capitalism which spews evil upon the population in return for massive profits. Those profits are then devoted to defrauding the voting population into installing autocrats who will, at a minimum, act to enhance the profits of the capitalists who are paying the politicians. This is all aided and abetted by religious institutions which seem more concerned with their cash flow than with the evil they are condoning in the process. Part of the fraud against the population is so-called "prosperity Gospel" where supposedly the Christian God wants you to make lots of money, and you make lots of money by engaging in immoral activities.

Even science has been infected by the immorality of modern capitalism. The tobacco industry and the fossil fuel industries each paid large sums to numerous scientists to defraud the public about the true evil being promulgated against them. Science is merely a process, and the people who "do science" can act for moral or immoral purposes. Knowing the truth doesn't imply moral action(s) in response.

We need an army of moral physicians to heal our society. In the process, we will give birth to a new civilization to replace the deathly and declining Western Civilization. It is long past its "sell by" date. Western Civilization has been declining for over two centuries, and the evil it now does is increasingly obvious.

Most people are not evil.[155] If people who are not inherently evil end up "doing evil" it is usually because they have been defrauded or misled into acting that way. And capitalism is a system designed to force the employees of a capitalistic company to do any evil as commanded by the management of the company for whom they work.

The root cause of evil in a capitalist economy is the focus on profit as the sole criterion for running a business enterprise. Profit is necessary, but evil is not. However, evil generally increases profit, unless it

---

[155] I suspect that the true quantity of evil people among us amounts to less than 10%. The word "most" is generally interpreted as "more than half." It is certainly the case that "more than half" of all people believe they are good people and would act appropriately if they knew the truth.

is "caught" in some costly way. Thus, business managers usually try to disguise their evil ways to avoid getting "caught" and then being forced to suffer a loss of profits to make right the evil they have done.

Unions provide a counterbalance to the evil of businesses but, as the history of the Teamsters Union clearly illustrates, a union isn't immune to the forces of evil. But a good union can do a lot to prevent evil by unionized businesses. Unions normally negotiate benefits for workers and the working conditions for workers. A good union contract prevents evil treatment of workers by the business. However, a corrupt union will allow the business to earn more profits by mistreating workers. And it is frequently difficult for the workers to know when their union has "sold them out" to their employers.

Evil is nothing if not inventive. Without moral constraints, evil will find a way to "do evil." That is just the nature of the game.

It is certainly the case that if we mount open action against evil, then evil will attack us in every possible way to preserve its profits (monetary or emotional).[156]. To avoid attacks to the maximum degree possible, we must act as an underground movement until we are in a position of a supermajority in some place. To accomplish this, I will form a series of institutions to shield our true activities from view by the public. The institutions I describe herein are just the first draft of what I believe is necessary. If it proves that other or additional institutions will be better, then we will do the better thing and not necessarily what I describe herein.

The overarching objective is to avoid evil as much as possible. Do not do evil to others unless necessary. Do not accept evil from others unless it is unavoidable. If the immoral capitalism of Western society is evil, and it surely is, then we should run our business affairs using principles of moral capitalism instead. This will be all about baby steps as people join our movement and contribute to its growth. The idea is to grow an "underground economy" that is run according to the principles of moral capitalism while also creating our own internal "welfare

---

[156] We should not forget that some people do evil things for the pure emotional joy of doing them.

state" which is supported by member contributions in the form of "church tithes."

We cannot afford to ignore the fact that evil people have taken control of governments around the world, including the government of the United States. Our affairs should be managed in such a way that we avoid, to the maximum extent possible, injuries due to an evil government choosing to take control of one or more of the institutions which we establish. We should maintain an "evil index" measuring the potential that a government might do evil against one or more of our institutions. Presently, nations like China, Russia, and North Korea would have the highest "evil index" values. It would be nearly impossible to establish a subculture of moral capitalism inside any of those nations. The other end of the scale may well be nations such as Switzerland and New Zealand. Global resources (ownership of institutions, funds in banks, significant valuables of any other type) should be in nations with the lowest "evil index" values. We should always remember that a large amount of wealth will be forever tempting to any autocrat who can choose to take control of that wealth.[157]

Every institution which we create should be under the moral control of the leadership body of the church which we establish. One way to maintain moral control while still accepting outsie investment can be done through a system of "golden shares" which have outsized voting power when moral judgements are involved.[158] Any such institution shall have at least one member of any board or committee running the institution, and that member can exercise the special voting rights to prevent doing evil. That should make it almost impossible for any of

---

[157] This is what is implied by Spengler's prediction of "the victory of force-politics over money." Once the autocrats decide that they can just take anything of value they wish, money no longer can control politicians or their actions. One example of how this might play out would be if Trump decided to merge NASA into SpaceX and put presidential appointees in charge of SpaceX. Maybe Musk would still own it, and maybe not (i.e., if the government paid him $0.10 on the dollar because "most of the value is from NASA") but either way, Trump would control it through the presidential appointees.

[158] Such shares are typically implemented as a special class, such as Class A shares having 10 times the voting rights of Class B shares. The idea here is that for the special purpose of declaring a moral principle which must be followed by the institution, the special class of shares will have voting rights sufficient to override the votes of all other classes of shares which might exist. Agnostic Church leaders will "have the gold" and make the rules.

our institutions to vote to "do evil" in any form (absent governmental interference requiring evil doing).

One thing I mentioned above is "church tithes." While our regular economic activities can be run in normal ways, to accumulate capital for new initiatives we should ask our church members to "tithe" a pledged amount into organizational growth funds. A church member would establish a monthly "tithe" and set the percentage to be given to each fund which that member wishes to support. Leadership at any level can establish a fund by creating a realistic budget to implement an idea. A small fund might create a local food bank or buy a small bus to use for group travel. A large fund might create a significant facility to use as a combination church and community center. People vote with their money to create one project or another out of the available proposals requesting contributions.

The remaining chapters discuss the three main organizations which I propose to create to implement this plan of action. The first, and broadest, Is the Good People Group (GPG).[159] Joining requires only a pledge to abide by the moral code defined by the Agnostic Church, as defined in prior portions of this book defining our moral principles. The second is the Agnostic Church itself. It is an actual church, where membership entails pledging money to the church. Meanwhile, the church uses its money to serve the needs of members through creating activities for the members to participate in. Just about anything any "mainstream" church has ever done is a candidate for an activity the Agnostic Church might do, except that any speeches would be under our dogmas and not promoting dogmas inconsistent with our dogmas. The third group is the Huxley Society, a lay leadership group to support and promote the Agnostic Church and the GPG. This will be a missionary team performing public service and recruiting converts.

---

[159] It is "broadest" in the sense that people can join GPG without any requirement to participate in any other activities. Once you commit to our value system, you can pick and choose what other activities to join.

To get things going, I've set up an online presence using my Agnostic Church domain name. Please join here:

https://www.agnostic.org/

(THIS PAGE IS INTENTIONALLY BLANK)

CHAPTER 10
GOOD PEOPLE GROUP

The subtitle of this book is "*Good People Banding Together.*" The Good People Group (GPG) is a collective of people who wish to form and participate in an underground economy for the mutual benefit of all. The phrase "Underground Economy" in this sense represents any form of moral capitalism which we practice amongst ourselves while excluding ourselves from the immoral capitalism of Western society. We band together to "do good" to each other for the mutual benefit of all. We can live according to our morality even if the rest of the society within which we live chooses to follow the immoral "vulture capitalism" of a dog-eat-dog zero-sum game.

One of the first businesses I would wish to establish is a credit union. The credit union, probably called the Huxley Credit Union, will serve the needs of anyone who belongs to our movement at any level (thinking of GPG as the first level, the Agnostic Church as the second level, and the Huxley Society as the third level). There should be one "legal entity" established for each regulatory jurisdiction (generally in the United States, that would mean at least one per US state). Additional legal entities could be established within a jurisdiction if geographic considerations would make that advisable.[160]

A credit union is the perfect vehicle to get away from the evil of the banking industry while still connecting to the electronic networks which make the modern economy function. Depending upon the laws governing credit unions in different places, I would hope to allow both individuals and small businesses to have accounts at the credit union. And a credit union decal in the window of a business would indicate to members that the business subscribes to our principles of moral capitalism in its business operations. Discounts would be offered to "Good People" who display valid membership cards in GPG or one of the

---

[160] An example of such a requirement might be the city of El Paso which is more than a day's drive from any other large city in Texas.

higher-level groups. Paying with a branded card could automatically trigger any applicable discount(s).

There are no limits to the kinds of business operations which can be accepted into the roster of moral capitalism. The main requirement shall be that charitable contributions must be made to activities established under the umbrella of the Agnostic Church. When enough money is available, an "affordable housing" subsidiary of the Agnostic Church would become a property developer in some communities, potentially developing "affordable housing" for either members or the public.[161] We need not follow the traditions of "stick built" homes, either. Innovation should be encouraged with new building materials and methods. It should be possible to assemble a home in a few days out of prefabricated parts rather than putting each piece in place at the building site.

Another example of moral capitalism is that we can be set up to help people who are unfairly or unjustly or randomly afflicted by circumstances. It is difficult to imagine the kinds of circumstances which might apply because they need to be evaluated on a case-by-case basis. But if somebody is a good person, and a member, we should take care of them in their hour of need. This could be as simple as finding them a room to inhabit within another member's home or making a small "loan of last resort" to help them through an unexpected financial difficulty.

Whatever we choose to do, the overarching idea is that **morality comes before profits**. We need profits to have funds available to help people, but we don't need profits for the sake of having more money at the end of the day — especially when those profits only serve to increase the wealth of those who are already extremely wealthy. **Ownership of money or things should never be the goal in life**; instead,

---

[161] It is a question to be asked as to whether we can give priority to our own members for the lease or purchase of "affordable housing" units which we construct using any kind of governmental subsidies.

money should be a way to **fund good in the world**, a principle recognized by many true philanthropists.[162]

We come into the world with **no money**, and we will take **none with us when we die** — even our funeral costs are the responsibility of those we leave behind. Our lives should be measured by **the good we do between birth and death**.

Will you join me in doing good?

To get things going, I've set up an online presence using my Agnostic Church domain name. Please join here:

https://www.agnostic.org/

---

[162] Who is a true philanthropist? https://givingpledge.org/ lists wealthy people who have signed up to "do good" with their wealth. Such people do exist.

(THIS PAGE IS INTENTIONALLY BLANK)

CHAPTER 11
AGNOSTIC CHURCH

Many years ago, I proclaimed myself to be the "Pope of the Agnostic Church." I still maintain an email address of **pope@agnostic.org**. The United States gives certain advantages to religious organizations, and the real purpose of the Agnostic Church is to avail ourselves of those advantages as we grow into a larger movement.

As we begin to organize ourselves into a new civilization (to replace Western Civilization), we will need a "church." We might as well use the Agnostic Church for all the purposes that any civilization needs a "church" as part of itself.

Finally, we can unite economically at lower cost if contributions are tax deductible because they are funneled through a church organization. For instance, the church can foster building homes, like what Habitat for Humanity does, but where the focus is providing living space for church members. Let the US tax code be our guide! Members in other nations would look to the laws of their own countries to figure out the best path forward in that place.

You might ask why "agnostic" instead of "atheist" in our name? There are a few reasons. First, the word "atheist" is frequently taken to mean "I don't believe in your God." While the word "agnostic" means the same thing, "agnostic" is less confrontational. We desire to make converts, so a less-confrontational approach is desirable. And while Bertrand Russell used both words to describe himself, he used the word "atheist" to ordinary people, but he used the word "agnostic" to audiences of professional philosophers because it was more defensible.

Second, both words require some definition of what "God" means before you can decide if you believe it or not.[163] Each person naturally begins by believing in whatever God or Gods they were taught about in their childhood. Almost all of humanity would agree that the Greek god Zeus does not exist because the religion of the ancient Greeks has

---

[163] This was a main point made by my friend Ted Drange in his book *Nonbelief & Evil: Two Arguments for the Nonexistence of God* (1998), Prometheus Press.

been largely not practiced for over 2,000 years. For that matter, that same reasoning would apply to any of the ancient Greek gods. The Christian idea of God has so many different versions, from the Bible literalist version to the Unitarian version, that it is impossible to make an argument for the nonexistence of all of them.

Throw in Christian concepts such as presuppositionalism and the argument becomes very difficult to "win" in formal debate sense.[164] But it only makes the Christians feel good since it is a fallacy and a "cheat" in a formal debate.

Third, atheism is seen as an affirmative claim, thus putting the burden of proof on the atheist in any debate. Agnosticism is a negative claim that swaps the burden of proof to the opposing debater. Again, for the sake of converting believers, agnosticism is a better starting point.

Fourth, agnosticism is the natural product of our way of knowing the truth. You admit that you don't know everything, so you should only assert knowledge which is supported by discernable facts and logical reasoning. There are many arguments to be made about the limits of human perception and Einstein's limit of the speed of light versus the size of the universe. Humans can't know anything about whatever is "outside" of the universe without an actual miracle to convey such knowledge.[165] Admitting a lack of knowledge is the best way to deal with these limitations.

The main purpose of the Agnostic Church is to provide moral leadership to the entire movement and whatever entities and groups are formed to assist group members. No person, however high up in movement leadership, should be incapable of being disciplined or removed

---

[164] Presuppositionalism is a Christian apologetic method that asserts that God must exist to even enable humans to think and so there is no foundation for any thought without God. Therefore, atheism is impossible. Presuppositionalism is an example of the "begging the question" fallacy (see the earlier chapter on logic). Thus, it is a fallacy, and a "cheat" to use it in a formal debate.

[165] This is where vocabulary begins to fail. There may be nothing "outside" of the universe. But, since the universe had a beginning, there was a pre-beginning "thing" out of which the universe was created by a process we do not understand but which we call the "Big Bang." At this point in time, the source of the "Big Bang" is a matter of pure speculation, and the concept of something existing "outside" of our universe is impossible to define let alone prove.

112

from their office(s) by an appropriate disciplinary council. In the same way, there should always be a defined line of succession in case of death, incapacity, or removal, to ensure the continuity of leadership in the movement.

To get things going, I've set up an online presence using my Agnostic Church domain name. Please join here:

https://www.agnostic.org/

(THIS PAGE IS INTENTIONALLY BLANK)

CHAPTER 12
HUXLEY SOCIETY

The Huxley Society will be organized as a secret society along the lines of many other such secret societies.[166] One example would be Freemasonry, sometimes called just the Masons.[167] A better example might be a society like the Knights of Columbus.[168] The Knights of Columbus is a particularly apt model as they are to the Catholic Church what the Huxley Society will be to the Agnostic Church. The main goal for the Huxley Society is to develop lay leaders who will promulgate the moral philosophy of the Agnostic Church within the wider society at large (all of what is now "the West") and take responsibility for recruiting new members for the Good People Group (GPG) and the Agnostic Church.

The goal will be to establish functioning chapters in every significant city and town where our movement is allowed to survive.[169] There will not be any inherent bias against any language, nationality, or ethnic group. If you can honestly subscribe to the principles and goals of the Huxley Society, you will be welcomed with open arms. What is required is belief in the philosophy and religious views outlined in this book. Typical of most secret societies, members will be initiated and work through a series of steps to gain access to the inner workings of the organization. The initiations will be designed to test the level of commitment and dedication to doing the work of the organization.

One goal would be to infiltrate existing institutions such as Boards of Education. With enough votes on school boards, this book can be

---

[166] See https://en.wikipedia.org/wiki/Secret_society for general information about secret societies.

[167] See https://en.wikipedia.org/wiki/Freemasonry_in_the_United_States for more on Freemasonry.

[168] See https://en.wikipedia.org/wiki/History_of_the_Knights_of_Columbus for more. Since the Knights of Columbus is associated with a particular religion, Roman Catholicism, it is a good model to look at for this purpose as we will need to promote the acceptance of our own religious views.

[169] Nations which are too far along the spectrum of authoritarian dominance will not allow us to survive. I expect Russia, China, Iran, North Korea, and any similar nations to be impossible to infiltrate openly. As the governance of other nations moves in the direction of authoritarian dictatorship, we must be alert to the possible need to move people and assets out of those nations before it is too late. The purpose of the "evil index" is to measure the level of preparation necessary, such as moving most of the money out of the country when the "evil index" is above some particular value.

made part of the curriculum. The idea would be to counter the moves in the arena of public schools to teach only those things useful to the common form of evangelical Christianity advocated by the authoritarians in charge. It is worth mentioning that the right is so afraid of secular education that a goal in red states is to impoverish public education, in part by diverting public money to fund private and/or Christian educational institutions, who use a curriculum more useful to the continued ignorance of the population. The Huxley Society should develop voluntary after-school programs and alternative private schools for our adherents and those who would seek to learn about us before joining. We need to plant our ideas into the minds of young people and allow those seeds to germinate as the children grow to maturity.

The primary purpose of the Huxley Society is to increase the membership numbers for the GPG and, by extension, the Agnostic Church. Of course, those activities should also lead to the growth of the Huxley Society itself. Growth should include fostering the creation of businesses to serve the needs of members. For instance, the Knights of Columbus offers insurance services and financial planning services. Any of the business functions mentioned for any of these organizations could be led by one or more members of the Huxley Society. We need to avoid over-expanding our operations, but we also need to foster growth.

The members of the Huxley Society should be the people who are most-dedicated to the goal of growing a new society out of the declining remnants of Western Civilization while, at the same time, easing the transition for as many people as possible.

To get things going, I've set up an online presence using my Agnostic Church domain name. Please join here:

https://www.agnostic.org/

INDEX

119

ABOUT BILL SCHULTZ

A disabled Vietnam veteran, serving from 1966 to 1974, Bill wrote his first computer program during a high school field trip. His long and varied career included highly classified work as a defense contractor, inventing microcomputer blade computing in 1978, creating a fiber to the home network in 1999, and over a decade working as a contractor and employee for cell phone companies. Along the way he joined groups of atheist and agnostic philosophers and worked to counter hatreds from the early days of the atheist movement.

(THIS PAGE IS INTENTIONALLY BLANK)

www.ingramcontent.com/pod-product-compliance
Lightning Source LLC
Chambersburg PA
CBHW071324130626
46556CB00004B/1728